How to Stop Worrying About Your Kids

How to Stop Worrying About Your Kids

✻✻✻✻✻✻✻✻✻✻✻✻✻✻✻✻✻✻✻✻✻✻✻

by J. D. SANDERSON

W · W · Norton & Company · Inc · *New York*

Copyright © 1978 by J. D. Sanderson
Published simultaneously in Canada by George J. McLeod Limited,
Toronto. Printed in the United States of America.
All Rights Reserved
First Edition

Portions of this book appeared in different form in the *Reader's Digest*
and the *New York Times*.

Library of Congress Cataloging in Publication Data

Sanderson, James Dean, 1925--
    How to stop worrying about your kids.

    1. Children—Management.   2. Adolescent psychology.
3. Young adults.   I. Title.
HQ772.S24   1978   649'.1   77-28091
ISBN 0-393-08808-1

Designed by Paula Wiener
1 2 3 4 5 6 7 8 9 0

Contents

My Daughter Wrote Me
a Letter on Father's Day...

Lisa had just graduated from high school a week earlier. On that warming June evening the purpose of our family dinner was less to celebrate Father's Day than to say goodbye to our oldest daughter, who was leaving the next day to find a summer job on Cape Cod before entering college in the fall.

She would be going alone—because a girl friend had changed her mind at the last moment. Lisa knew no one on the Cape, had no idea where she would be staying, and everyone had warned her that the best jobs would be taken. To the world she was a tall, well-developed girl with long black hair and a confident smile—a near-woman. To us, caught up in the memories of only yesterday, she seemed something less. Could we really let this "baby" walk away into the real world, so casually and so alone?

But that night after dinner, after the traditional Father's Day lemon pie she had helped bake, Lisa gave me a present. It was a letter, accompanied by a shy kiss. And that's how my wife and I finally came to *know*.

DEAR DAD,

What can I give you on Father's Day? I'm too old for little presents with little messages, and so I thought I would give you something that you taught me—writing—and in this writing tell you all the other things you've taught and given me.

I have no distinct first memory of you, but Mommy tells me that you and I used to go out on the roof in Greenwich Village and look at the moon and stars, and I would point to the moon and say, "moon-a." I was a little self-centered then, too, thinking because Lisa ended with an "A" every other word in the world did also.

I remember a talk we had when I was eight or nine up in your room. We were talking about Mommy and you told me how selfish you and I were and how patient and giving Mommy was. And it struck me, even then, how someone as old as you were could admit something like that to a child. So few parents *ever* admit that they are wrong about anything, much less admit a personal fault; and it's too bad because then their children never learn to, either. Admitting you are wrong or are not perfect is very important in learning to get along with people and being honest with yourself. Looking back on it now, I could not agree that you are a selfish man.

Another distinct memory I have is of your going to Immaculate Conception School when I was in second grade, to ask them not to make me eat lunch. How ridiculous I was! But you didn't think so, and you went and must have been very embarrassed. Most parents would have thought it would have been good for me—maybe cure me of being such a picky eater—but you didn't think of what would be easiest for you, you thought about *me*.

I remember I used to dread letting you go over my school reports, especially in high school, because it invariably meant doing them over. But you taught me a valuable lesson: never accept mediocrity in your work or your ambition. Although that can be a great burden, generally it's a good thing. Unfortunately, a dislike for mediocrity in others goes along with it and that can be a great burden for your friends unless you learn to accept people pretty much as they are.

Once you told me in Junior High (when we went out to celebrate right after my opening in "Bye Bye, Birdie") that you thought I was balanced right in the middle. You said either I would just get married or that I would really go out and achieve something on my own—you couldn't decide which. Right then and there I decided that I wouldn't *just* get married. Marriage was important but it wouldn't be the only goal in my life. I'm glad you've made me ambitious.

You have made me so strong and secure in myself that unlike other kids I'm not afraid to go out on my own now and start my life. I know you've taught me all the basics, in the most painless way, and I'm sure I will be able to deal with what's ahead. Dennis asked me the other day why I planned never to come back to Montclair and work or "settle down." Then you could be near your parents when they need you, he said. And I answered all they need is for me to go out and become a success-ful person—that's all they ever wanted from me and that's the best thing I can do for them. Happy Father's Day, Dad.

Your loving daughter,
LISA

I read Lisa's letter aloud at the table. When I was finished, the two younger children stared first at me and then at Marion to see whether we thought this "gift" was appropriate. They were sur-prised to see tears in both of us. *Was there ever a gift so magnificent?* As we hugged Lisa, Marion and I looked at each other and knew that we had nothing to worry about. Our child would leave home the next morning and she would not only survive in the outer world, she would flourish. For that summer, and in college, and for the rest of her life. A tidal wave of awe swept over us that, somehow, every-thing had "worked out all right." She was eighteen and, incredibly, she was an Adult. She not only understood us—she understood herself. And our job was done, as far as any parent ever could do it.

We felt a giddy relief, of the kind that parents used to talk about when they saw their daughter married off to a strong young man with good prospects. We also felt an instant surge of pleasure in recognizing that we could welcome her not only to the secrets of adulthood but also to the rank of friend. We could *enjoy* her more. Blood of our blood, creature of our care, participant in the dramas and ennuis of our daily life for eighteen years, the re-creation of ourselves and yet something totally different: a marvelous human being now capable of responding at the highest level and enlarging *us* as she grew beyond whatever we had given her.

It is very trendy to say that this just can't happen, that parents can't lead and children won't follow and that we are all mired together in the swamps of change and uncertainty. Novelist Anne Roiphe, writing in the *New York Times Magazine*, says she has a friend who assigns all the people she knows into two categories: those who believe that with hard work and good intentions everything will work out, and those who believe that life is a series of random disasters, entirely unrelated to our ideals or our actions. The people in the first category, she says, invariably have *small* children; those in the second are parents of teenagers or older children.

Now, this brings a certain amused smile, but Anne Roiphe, herself a mother, tops it with what could be the punchline for a *New Yorker* cartoon. An older man walking off a tennis court at Nantucket turns to the younger man who has just beaten him and says: "You play a good game, but it's only because your children haven't betrayed you yet."

We can laugh—with a gasp of recognition. All parents live in uncertainty, not in what they know to be right but in how to apply it in specific instances. In Wall Street there is a saying that it is easy to buy good stocks but nobody ever rings a bell to tell you when to sell. In parenting, all of us set up our principles and attempt to apply them, but few bells are ever rung to tell us whether the thing is working or not. Nevertheless, most of us *don't* feel that our kids are "betraying" us. They aren't becoming drug addicts or teen alcoholics or high school dropouts or runaways or religious freaks, and they don't need an abortion. Yes, we all know of instances, but for every one of these we can count up ten who aren't going to get into serious trouble, because their parents aren't going to let conditions arise in a child's life which would lead to this kind of disaster.

It's the damned uncertainty, though, which plagues us. On that

Father's Day night Marion and I immediately began to worry about our *other* children. All parents marvel at the astonishing differences in their offspring—maybe we'd just been lucky with Lisa. Maybe she was one of these rare human spirits who come out a winner no matter what rearing they have. What about Eric and what about Eve?

Well, that was nearly five years ago. Lisa has not only confirmed the promise she gave in her letter but our other two children seem to be developing just fine. As far as we can tell they are also on schedule to become fully functioning Adults at Eighteen. The fact that we have set a deadline—their eighteenth birthday—has removed a good deal of uncertainty in their minds and ours as to who has to do what by what date. No children grow up until the facts of life require them to; Marion and I have simply decided that we aren't going to sit around fingering our worry beads waiting for sudden dawning on their part. *We* are the facts of life right now, and if we are satisfied that our children can handle themselves emotionally and intellectually and financially at age eighteen, the world will be too.

This book actually began with a series of long letters to Lisa as a college freshman. Because of the response by some of her friends, Lisa encouraged me to develop the ideas into a book, in which a father explains to his daughter what the real world is all about. I was half through the first draft and even had a title, "Sweet Daughter, How I Love Thee . . ." But then I bogged down. Finally my wife said, "You are trying to tell these girls things their own fathers should have explained. The book you really want to write is aimed at the fathers, to show them they can get involved with their kids at an earlier age."

She was right. I knew I wanted to talk about sons as well as daughters, and I wanted to say to fathers that no matter what their role in the family in the pre-teen years, they are terribly needed now—and the Adult at Eighteen timetable will help to make them more comfortable and hopeful in trying to impose some developmental structure on the teen world. And also that the very process of getting involved in this way will change how a man thinks about his own life—about his wife, his job, his money, and his retirement.

But this is not a "father" book. In most families the mother lives closer to the child, day after day, and if she isn't in full agreement with her husband no bright ideas of his are going to speed the children to Adulthood. When it comes to the teen years, it's a full and equal collaboration of both parents, or it's nothing.

I want to emphasize that Adult at Eighteen is a long-term effort beginning in the *early* teen years. When portions of this book appeared in *Reader's Digest* and the *New York Times*, some readers wrote in to protest. Usually their children were already in full rebellion against parents and environment, and thus the approaches suggested here seemed unrealistic and much too tame. In other cases the children were already over eighteen and still struggling to find themselves; but obviously the things you can say to kids of thirteen or sixteen may be totally inappropriate when the children are nineteen or twenty-three.

This book is not therapy and it contains no instant magic. It is simply one way for a father and mother to organize their thinking about the parental function while they still have time to exercise some authority. When a child is finished with high school it is usually too late to do much more than wish him or her well.

We've all read too many articles and books which talk in generalities about raising kids. As the old farmer told the young salesman who was pressuring him to buy an encyclopedia of farming: "Son, I don't need any more books. I already ain't farming half as well as I know how."

For this reason this book is the personal story of how my wife and I have tried to lead and prod our kids to some kind of tentative maturity. To see someone else's daily struggle may be more helpful than all the "encyclopedias" we understand but can't apply.

We are not an average family—no family is. But I doubt you will find our problems or our aspirations very different from your own. What you will see here, I hope, is simply the application of the plain middle-class values and common sense which most parents share. As Oliver Wendell Holmes said, "We need education in the obvious more than investigation of the obscure."

How to Stop Worrying About Your Kids

1 ✳

The human race marks time, century after
century, because the generations learn
nothing from each other if they are given
the freedom to refuse to learn.
—Pearl Buck

Parents Get the Kind of Kids They Deserve

We parents are only human, and so we are very good at rationalizing about our kids. At any stage in their development we are able to convince ourselves that it isn't totally our fault when things go wrong. Some kids seem to be born not only with beauty but strength, wisdom, and mysterious talents; some kids appear to have none, and it doesn't seem to be our *fault*. The times are all wrong, anyway. Parental authority has been destroyed. Our society is corrupt, and often the environment we have to live in is savage. The schools are incompetent, our churches irrelevant, and above all the pressures of life today rob us of time and psychic energy to such an extent that we have trouble getting through our own adult day.

All parents go through these midnight despairs, and Marion and I have had our share. But the next morning we realize that it was just another temporary failure of the flesh, and we can't cop out on our kids any more than we can throw up our hands and say our own lives are such a mess that nothing can be done.

Deep within we know what nature assigned us to do. The young must be taught what they need to know to survive, and if this is a tougher job than it used to be because our society is more complex and is changing so rapidly, then all the more reason to make

15

a conscious, organized effort to cope with the problem. For a long time we parents have been trying to delegate important portions of our role to the social institutions around us, but when these fail we have to gather the reins of authority back into our own hands. These days if we don't bring our children to safe maturity nobody else will—*or can*.

What do we need to do the job? Just three things:

1. The ability to express love and offer emotional support in a constant daily flow no matter what adversities strike us inside or outside the relationship with the child.

2. The courage to believe, from the moment of conception to the child's eighteenth birthday, that we *can* impart our values and some parts of our experience, that we can *succeed* in giving this creature of our selves a separate and functioning adulthood.

3. The faith that we can instill the best of what we are (and not the worst) into our offspring, so that we find ourselves in the rather odd, joyous position of trying to live up to the image we would have our child see and model himself after.

Now, it is easy to love a small child, and to swell with aspiration about what we are going to do for this child. But as the birthdays rocket past us with ever-increasing speed, the job gets harder. It gets so complicated, in fact, that we become confused and frightened, even terrified at forces unleashed and apparently out of control. We lose our courage and our faith, if not our love; bit by bit we give up. The saddest of all parental songs is, "I did my best—it wasn't my fault."

This is the reason I believe that when a child enters the teen years, as just the stage when everything seems to be falling apart on both sides, the parents must sit down together and organize a *plan* for the child's final development. The plan must have a time limit if it is going to be realistic. One reason parents stumble is that the parenting job seems to go on *forever*. When are we finally finished—when a child marries and moves far away? Are we through even then? Few of us are getting younger and the frustrations and failures in our own lives have taken their emotional toll.

Some children seem to be a kind of life sentence; who can blame us if we try to evade the full implication of it?

But if we say, my child is now thirteen or fourteen . . . I have just five (or four) years to complete the job—to do *everything* I am going to do for this creature of mine—so, yes, I can summon up the strength to cope. It's now or never—I can see my child through this far at least. All of us feel a marvelous release when we put a deadline on any job. In this case the urgency we bring to the effort excites and galvanizes not only our energies but those of the child. Something is *happening*, somebody has taken charge!

Adult at Eighteen . . . What do I mean by this? It is a planned effort by the parents to relinquish Authority over the child, area by area, as the youngster assumes the necessary Responsibility, until at the child's eighteenth birthday or graduation from high school (whichever comes first) the son or daughter is not only fully competent to leave home but is eager to do so. At this point *all* authority and responsibility have been transferred to the new adult, for better or for worse.

At our house we have a Family Conference about every six months to discuss all the ways in which we are living together. We try to make it an important occasion. The date is announced well in advance, so nobody has to cut short the discussion because of other obligations. We generally go out to dinner first to put everybody in a good mood, but if, for some reason, any member of the family is upset or clearly resistant, the family conference is postponed for a few days.

Here is the way the concept of Adult at Eighteen was introduced most recently, as we all sat around the dining-room table. Both Marion and I, of course, had agreed on all matters ahead of time.

Adult at Eighteen—How It Begins

"Well, Eve became a teenager last week, and we were happy to see this happen because now she has begun the final stage of growing to adulthood. We can start giving her more freedom and responsibility, and stop treating her like a child. When we were growing up the law said you weren't an adult until you reached twenty-one, but recently the Constitution was amended—reducing the age of majority to eighteen. Hardly anybody in the country opposed this change, because most parents felt you kids today are smarter and more mature than we were. You know more about the world and how to get along in it than we did at your age.

"And so just five years from now you are going to be completely in charge of yourself. You can vote for public officials and serve on juries; you can borrow money from a bank; you will be able to buy and sell property; people can sue you; in most states you can walk into a bar or liquor store without question, and no one will stop you from getting drunk; you can get married without asking our permission; if you get in trouble with the law you'll be put in prison, not sent to a juvenile home; you can get an abortion; you will have full freedom to do any kind of work, and spend your money any way you see fit. You will choose your own career, and decide whether or not to go to college; but when you graduate from high school it will be up to you to earn your own living—we will no longer support you. You will have to set up your own home or apartment, and find a good enough job to pay the rent and buy your own food."

By now you are receiving the child's full attention. It has not really dawned on him or her that the pleasant protected cocoon of childhood might not go on forever. The child is suddenly apprehensive, and this is a necessary shock to set the Adult process in motion. The older children too, even though they have heard these words before, suddenly begin to wonder anew just what you mean by it all. Are you really going to "kick them out of the house"? Are you withdrawing all support? Have you stopped caring about them and loving them?

No, of course not, and you have to say *very clearly* that this isn't what you mean by growing up.

"We love you more than anything else in the world, and we always will—even when you get to be sixty years old. There isn't anybody in the world we could ever love more—you are our *children*, you are part of us. You have given us so much love and satisfaction and pleasure that we couldn't bear to give that up. We aren't suddenly going to rent your room out to a stranger; your room will always be there and you can come home to visit any time you want to. The most fun we can have will be having you come back to see us. But the point is, if we do our job right in the next five years and you do your job of growing up, you'll be eager to get out on your own when you're eighteen—just as Lisa is. You'll be fed up with living at home and you'll want to have your own place with total freedom to come and go as you like, to eat and work and play without us looking over your shoulder, to make all your own decisions and build your own life as you see it. You know, Eve, we come from another generation, and no matter how loving and understanding we try to be, we're never going to see things exactly the way you do. You may be more right than we are about how you should live your life, but you'll never have full control over *everything* until you move out of this house."

These are just words, really, at this point; the child is still worried. So immediately you must point out some tangible benefits the teen will receive in working toward the Adult goal. This is what we said to Eve:

"Five years may seem like a long time to you, but you'll be surprised how soon they'll pass. We have a lot to get done before that time, so right now here are four areas in which we are going to stop treating you like a child, if you feel you can handle the responsibility.

"1. The first thing we're going to do is take down that poster in the hall near your room. You know, the World War I recruiting picture of a stern Uncle Sam pointing a finger out at you saying 'WE WANT YOU . . . to Clean Up Your Room!' Yes, believe it or not, we're going to stop bugging you about your room. We're never going to say another word no matter how messy your room gets (although we may ask you to close the door so we don't have to look at it). Most of your life you're going to be living with someone; if you go to college you'll certainly have a roommate, and you'll probably have a husband someday. If you go on living in a sty you're going to drive them crazy; they're going to start thinking of you as a pig, and worst of all you may start feeling that way about yourself. But you know all this. So from now on it's your problem—we've got more important things to talk to you about.

"2. Similarly, we're going to stop worrying about your personal grooming. When you were a child we had to remind you to brush your teeth and comb your hair and clean your fingernails. But one adult doesn't have to do that for another. Your mother is not going to lay out clean underwear or advise you what clothes to wear in the morning—in fact, except for Christmas she isn't going to select any of your clothes any more. It's up to you to pick up your clothes from the floor and put them in the laundry basket, so that you have a fresh supply; and if you don't have enough clothes it's up to you to ask either of us to take you over to the shopping mall. We're going to let you make all the decisions on clothes, even if we think you're making a mistake. We won't offer any advice unless you ask us.

"3. We are no longer going to tell you what time to go to bed. Equally, we are only going to call you once in the morning; if you are so tired that you oversleep and miss the bus we are not going to drive you to school ever again. You will have to ride your bicycle, even if it makes you late. At this age you know how many hours of sleep you need to function well the next day, and it's up to you to get those hours. Small children have to be tucked in, but how can we ever expect you to be an adult if we go on nagging you about going to bed? You are an attractive girl, and I think you know what lack of sleep is going to do to your looks, as well as your schoolwork. Do you think you can handle this?

"4. You have studied nutrition in health class and you know about the different groups of foods you should eat each day in order to have a proper diet. So we are going to stop worrying about whether you eat your carrots or spinach or whatever. We expect you to get up in the morning in time to eat at least part of the breakfast your mother fixes for you. At noon you are on your own, both at school and at home. At night we expect you to sit at the dinner table and to eat at least part of what food is put before you. If you persist in chucking down all those goodies after school, we're simply going to cut down on the amount of junk food and desserts that we buy, but we aren't going to nag you about it. A child has to be fed, but an adult takes care of her own diet. The vitamin pills are in plain sight on the breakfast bar; we expect you to act in a responsible way in the future about the food and drink you put into your mouth."

These are brave words, and the biggest problem is for the parents to mean them. Does the child accept the offer? Yes, the child is flattered and pleased with his new liberty. Does he act responsibly, as a result? No, of course not. Unless you can say it in a more persuasive manner than we ever did, there is no change in behavior at all. Not right away, anyway. What does happen is a change in *perception*. The child senses that some process has been put in motion; he * dimly begins to see a path leading somewhere up over a steep hill into the mist of maturity. Some unexpected concessions have been made, for which he is grateful; but at the same time some new kinds of demands have been placed, and these make him a little uneasy. He no longer has the exquisite luxury of perfect passive resistance—of waiting until a course of action is proposed for every detail of his life and then vetoing it if it seems inconvenient. He now has to think about his needs occasionally, and make some proposals to himself.

When a child is in the womb he is the center of the universe and all of his sustenance is supplied automatically. In middle-class American families the condition of the womb is often nearly dupli-

* No sexism should be inferred. Used in this context, "he" obviously means "he or she." English may be the most flexible language in the world but it still lacks a good, short, third-person pronoun covering both genders.

cated for most of a child's life. At age thirteen a small blast of cold air has to be let in. A child has to begin to see that he isn't at the center of the universe anymore, and that not all of his needs are going to be tended automatically.

How many kids do you know in their late teens or even their early twenties who still haven't gotten this message?

2 ✻

Reducing the Level
of Confrontation

Marion and I decided that we had a second and equally important reason why we had to "let go" in these four areas (just as a starter). We had to find ways to stop quarreling with our kids.

As an experiment, carry a note pad with you for one twenty-four-hour period and keep a record of each communication you have with each child. I can't tell you how shocked I was to discover that 95 percent of the times I spoke to my daughters or my son I was correcting, admonishing, criticizing, or ordering something done. I was often so annoyed (if not angry) that I had no time or desire to express approval or love. No wonder they don't want to listen to us! It's always bad news.

A friend of mine says that passive resistance was not invented by Mahatma Gandhi but by the American teenager. Any human constantly under attack has to resist to survive, and our kids resist by turning off, by not listening, by "forgetting," or simply by ignoring us.

By the age of thirteen or fourteen our children have heard us; they just haven't chosen to acknowledge it. They know exactly what we are talking about and how we feel about every aspect of our daily routine, and may even agree with us. Then why won't they do what we ask them to? Because (a) it is pleasant not to give up instant gratifications, and (b) they are angry at being constantly harassed about matters which don't seem that important to them, and (c) they are trying to find a way to separate themselves from their parents, to express their individuality; and that's not so easy these days.

Every parent must say: I've got to stop fighting with my kids about the routine aspects of life which really don't matter. If I'm constantly in a state of Confrontation, how can I ever talk to them about subjects that are important, such as boy-girl relationships, drugs, emotional problems, school, cultural development, career choices, happiness? My kids know all about going to bed and eating meals, but they're very uncertain about those other areas. If that's where they're going to need my help, it's important to do whatever is necessary right now to open up the channels so they will not only listen but will actually seek advice and help.

A parent doesn't ever have to surrender his standards. Our children know how we feel about keeping that room in a state of non-shambles, for example, and we can quietly remind them once in a while that our views haven't changed. But we have shifted the responsibility to them, and we have to stick with the decision that we aren't going to confront them in this area—no matter how bad things get. We should understand that we have already managed to instill a considerable amount of *guilt* in the child, if our standard has been reasonable. He or she knows we are right, and knows it would be better to do what we suggest. Sooner or later, as the teen gets older and the relationship improves, he will respond in some of these areas of daily life (but probably not all of them). Common sense develops in the young along with the other faculties.

For some time, however, it's going to look as if the system isn't working at all, so once in a while we have to remind them of the agreement: "Look, we're trying to treat you with respect in this family, like one adult to another. We don't want to order you around—adults don't do that to one another. But you agreed to take on the responsibility for getting to bed early enough so you could function at school, and you're failing that responsibility. You're so exhausted in the morning that you can hardly open your eyes. I don't know how you can keep awake all day. Now, when you were a child we told you when to get undressed, when to brush your teeth, and we turned off the lights in your room. You surely don't expect us to go back to that? OK? Do you think you can function as an adult in this area in the future? There's a lot more freedom we want to give you—more than other kids get—so when you say you can handle it we count on you to do it."

Adult at Eighteen: The Second Family Conference

Six months later you should, of course, begin by praising any progress each child has made in assuming greater responsibility. Be gentle about failures; restate your position calmly. In our family each sibling is quick to point out the other's failures, and our job, often enough, is to prevent the victim from feeling he is being ganged up on. In attacking the problem of psychological resistance it is also important to reduce the level of confrontation between the kids themselves.

The real purpose of the second conference, however, is to identify the remaining areas of daily routine which stir constant conflict between parent and child. Ask for suggestions from the kids: in what new ways can we give up exercising authority over you while you assume the responsibility for yourself? If you can elicit any response at all you have taken a major step in making your children see that the process is moving ahead toward the final goal of Adult at Eighteen. Accept any suggestion with praise and see if you can lay out the ground rules to make it work.

Every family is different, obviously; but here are some further "daily routine" problems that we had to work through in our house before we could begin to talk to each other in a reasonable way.

CHORES: We explained that our family is really just like a "commune." Everybody contributes what he can to the effort to keep the group going and takes out from the commune what he needs to sustain his life. So far, however, mother and father have done all the work, and the kids have simply taken, and that isn't fair. If the kids join a counter-culture commune they won't be able to do that—the others will insist that they do their share. And they will actually *want to*, so they feel they belong.

"Yes, each of you kids has had some chores assigned to you before," we say, "but there has been too much fighting and resistance about that. So we are going to start over. We aren't going to ask you to contribute money to the commune, but here is a list of the work that needs to be done. All of these jobs you either know how to do or we can teach you how very quickly, so forget your past chores and volunteer now to make a contribution to the commune that is important and really needed." For example:

> Running the washing machine and dryer once a week.
> Sorting and returning clean clothes to individuals.
> Vacuuming the house once a week.
> Grocery shopping from a list once a week.
> Cooking dinner one night per week.
> Clearing the dinner table at night.
> Washing dishes.
> Emptying the dishwasher.
> Taking out the garbage.
> Washing the car.
> Mowing lawn—shoveling snow.
> Doing all other needed yardwork.
> Total responsibility for family pets.
> Washing windows.
> Waxing floors.

One reason so many kids feel alienated from their families is that they are never required to become members. They are free boarders, nothing less, and rather critical and disdainful boarders at that. It requires a heap of work to make a house a home, and lots of it is physical. Wouldn't you think this is one of the most elementary facts of life that a parent could teach a child? We had to experience a certain shock before we got the message, as witness the following conversation:

MOTHER: It takes you an hour to rinse off some dishes and load them in the dishwasher.

THIRTEEN-YEAR-OLD: Why should I have to do the dishes every night? I'm not a slave, you know.

MOTHER: If you don't do the dishes, who should?

THIRTEEN: You.

MOTHER: I'm not a slave, either.

THIRTEEN: Who says?

There it is; the word popped right out. Now, obviously this is merely the tip of an attitudinal iceberg, and unless the parents come to grips with it, this child is going to have lots of trouble during the teen years and beyond. The family is the first and most important group that a child belongs to; he *must* have the experience of contributing to the work of the group. It is the most elementary lesson in learning that you never get something for nothing, in learning to do something for others, in learning to work together, in learning to perceive the problems of others. In the process, a child may even acquire a few useful skills. When a boy goes off to college, who's going to do his laundry? Let him learn how to push a button on a washing machine. Let him learn how to make a simple meal: what's so tough about grilling a hamburger, opening a package of frozen vegetables, and baking a potato?

If a mother works, obviously everybody in the family including the father has to share in the household duties. If she doesn't work, the arrival of teen birthdays should still herald the beginning of Mother's Liberation. She should insist on substantial help from teen children as she begins to plant the seeds of her Second Life, which should come to full flower when the last child reaches eighteen.

CHILD TRANSPORTATION: The second Family Conference should certainly make decisions about family mobility. It's not only demoralizing for Mother to constantly interrupt her life to chauffeur kids around, it also perpetuates an infantile attitude in the kids. We have a flat rule that if any teen *can* get where he needs to go on his own he *will* do so. He will walk, he will take public transport, he will ride his bicycle—even in bad weather. And this includes girls. No point within the boundaries of our town is more than five miles from our house; thus, on a ten-speed bike, everything is accessible within a half hour's ride. In fact, most of the shopping and recreation areas the kids want to go to are only ten or fifteen minutes away by bicycle.

Yes, there are certain risks, but we spend some time working on bicycle safety. If a teen can't handle a bicycle on city streets, how's he ever going to manage with a car? We do have some concern about riding after dark, and in the early teen years we do continue to drive at night if the activity is essential and beyond walking distance. But we take a jaundiced view of that word "essential." Any teen who wants to see a movie with his friends during vacation, for example, can schedule it during daylight hours rather than at night when he would have to be chauffeured.

In the beginning every teen sees the removal of the instant chauffeur as a grave injustice, and parents often succumb to the begging, whining, and bluster. It really doesn't seem that much extra trouble to hop in the car one more time, especially when the weather isn't perfect. But if you are trying to teach a would-be adult the joy of independence, you have to give him his own legs, and require him to exercise them whenever possible. A teen needs the pride of coming and going without constant parental supervision.

EARNING MONEY: Since we live in the greatest consumer society man has ever known, it's not surprising that our kids are insatiable in their material demands. This has to be settled very early in the teen years or even before, and it can be decided in only one way: If you want it, earn it. When Lisa was about six we decided she should have some experience in handling money, so we offered her an allowance of 25 cents a week. The days of penny candy were long gone even then, but it was still great fun to see her with her nose pressed up against the glass case in our nearby soda shop, agonizing over a packet of bubble gum vs. a Baby Ruth. When she was ten the allowance was raised to 50 cents, and at thirteen to one dollar a week. That's as high as it ever went. Well into high school she complained that her friends were drawing two-, three-, and even five-dollar allowances, but we had decided that the experience of managing money could only be valuable at this stage if she earned it herself. (Logically we should have dropped the allowance altogether, but we decided not to make an issue out of one dollar a week.)

Every person derives a large measure of his sense of worth from the work that he does. School, of course, is a child's "work," and all parents try to give their children pride based on their achievements there. But school often doesn't seem "real" to a child—it's something kids do. Grownups work for *money*—and so the real world starts, in some respects, when someone in the outside world is willing to put spendable cash into their hand in return for a job well done.

I can still remember Eve's first baby-sitting job. She was eleven and had worried for weeks that our neighbor thought she was still too much of a baby herself to let her sit even for an hour after school. Then one day the call finally came and she was in a panic. *Would* she be able to handle the job? Well, of course she did. That night at dinner the three quarters she had earned were arranged in a neat row beside her plate, and the glow of pride which suffused her face told us that we had just witnessed an important rite of passage.

Every parent has a memory or two like this. The value of the work experience to a young person is so obvious that parents ought not only to encourage the idea but to insist on it. This means that except for Christmas and birthdays you don't hand out presents, and you don't give them cash for anything except the reasonable necessities of life. Allowances should be minimal, and parents should take whatever steps necessary to open doors to the widest possible variety in work experience. This is not simply for the money, but to expose the teen to the real-life demands of other adults.

Parents can preach the adult virtues, but it is often outsiders, even strangers, who enforce our vision. They are the ones who *finally* convince a teenager that he must be on time, he must be courteous, he must dress and act appropriately, he must listen to instructions, he must be attentive, he must follow the job through to completion—and clean up afterwards. And, quite often, outsiders convince the teen that if he injects some extra effort and thought into his job he will receive valuable praise, and maybe even a tip or bonus.

What kind of work should he do? It doesn't matter. Each new challenge he meets provides new confidence and new pride—it's more satisfying than any kind of play. A disaffected teen, almost by definition, is a kid with an inadequate work experience. He hasn't met enough strange adults who as a matter of course require him to think and act in a responsible way, and he doesn't know that he can.

Well, those were our first priorities on the teen road toward Adult at Eighteen. Take care of your own quarters, dress yourself, feed yourself, go to bed and get up by yourself, transport yourself as often as you can, see yourself as a part of the family to the extent that you share the routine maintenance, and earn your own spending money outside the home. Obviously these are only the most elementary transition points between dependence and autonomy, but if you can't make some progress along these external lines at age thirteen or fourteen, when are you going to be able to get to the real business of growing up?

What *is* the real obligation of parents? It is to create a sense of inner worth in the child, a sure knowledge that the outside world is not so complicated or frightening that he can't cope. Like master masons, parents must construct layer after layer of ego strength, teaching a child that he can think and act and take, while at the same time perceiving and *feeling* the needs of others and giving back. Loving and being loved.

Does all this require some kind of genius on the part of the parents? Certainly not. There are too many variables not subject to our control. We are only required to produce at eighteen a *reasonably* competent adult. Every human must ultimately resolve his own troubles in life; we are only responsible for giving our children some basic equipment to do it.

Despite our brave words during the first two Family Conferences, did we achieve instant success in our family? Ah, no. We saw constant relapses, and Marion and I felt our moments of depression all the way up to the eighteenth birthday, and beyond. But it is the natural condition of parents to feel frustrated most of the time about their children. We had to keep telling each other: Let's not lose our nerve, let's just keep plugging away at what we know to be right. We've got a plan, so let's honor it. Let's focus on the basics of human behavior so consistently that our children cannot escape. Our kids don't have to be perfect at eighteen—we just have to have some strong evidence they're going to survive and grow into decent human beings.

3 ✳

They Need More Love
Than We Think

Every parent sees himself as overflowing with love for his children. Why else would we work so hard to feed, clothe, and look after them? Why else would we spend so much time thinking about them and *worrying* about them? Surely our kids must know that we care enormously; how could they not know it? We have been telling them we love them since the very moment of birth, and even before.

But have we, really? When was the last time we actually said "I love you" out loud, with our arms around them? Did we do it today? Last week? Maybe—just maybe—we have been internalizing this love instead of demonstrating it, especially as our children move into the teen years. We can remember how we hugged and kissed them, but can they?

Every human has an insatiable need for approval and reassurance. If even as adults we can never get enough, how much more intense the needs of our growing children! They frequently act so "cool," assured, and even cocky that we allow ourselves to forget. Or, more honestly, we permit ourselves to overlook for a time the needs we really know about, because it is simply too difficult to break through their shell to the soft part. If we are having adult troubles of our own—and who isn't?—we frequently can't get up the energy it takes to achieve an emotional breakthrough with our kids.

Nevertheless, if we expect our children to be truly stable, self-sufficient adults by eighteen, we have got to register our love and approval in unmistakable terms. Both parents have to find a way to do it *nearly every day* through the teen years. How can our children become strong and independent unless they believe they can? In today's world, parents are the chief reliable source of the "emotional supplies" necessary to build and reinforce this belief.

A teenager's view of how we love him may be quite different from our own. When we reproach him for not getting his homework done or not practicing the piano on schedule, we see it as an act of *caring*. But he may view it as just one more personal attack and, subconsciously, as another reason why we are disappointed in him, one more proof that he is unworthy. When we tell him to be home at a certain hour at night, we express a concern for his safety; but the teen may see it as lack of faith in his ability to physically take care of himself or to meet his or her moral responsibilities.

A parent's love should be as warm and as unconditional as the sunshine, and should be perceived as such. This means that we have to find ways of touching, ways of saying what we feel, which are totally divorced from our daily routine of teaching and correcting. We have a hundred different reasons to be angry at our sons and daughters for the actions they take, or fail to take; and often, without realizing it, we use a diminished display of love as a disciplinary tactic.

Of course this is wrong; we should never be angry at the child himself, only at the action or the failure. All of us find it very difficult to make this separation; we often feel so powerless in dealing with our children that we believe an emotional explosion is the only way to get through to them, to show that we feel *strongly* about something. And, to tell the truth, we often are not sufficiently in control of ourselves to resist this direct attack on the child. Sometimes, too, we vent the accumulated frustrations and angers of our adult lives simply because the lapses of our children have provided a seemingly legitimate opening for these feelings to be released.

Yes, we all *know* this. And we try to work on it—we try not to blow up. But the anger is still there, in a word, a gesture, a set of the mouth. We want them to do something and they *won't* and we're sore about it, and they get defensive and try to avoid contact, which only annoys us more. Sometimes the process goes on for days, or even weeks, and it becomes psychologically impossible for us to throw our arms around a teen and say, "Sweet daughter, I love you so much," or "Son, I'm so proud of you." We *can't* say that because we are in a confrontation; we're afraid that any gesture like this might be viewed as a signal that we've surrendered. And since we usually feel we're fighting for principle, we can't bear to surrender.

What can we do to prevent this? Very simply, we have to say to ourselves: "My number one priority as a mother or as a father is *not* to discipline my child today. It is to express love and approval, either through words or physical touching, or both. I will find a way to do this no matter how I feel about my child's conduct or attitude, because I know he needs this reassurance desperately, and I need to remind myself how much I love him. And once we have got this clear in our heads again, we may be able to work out the disciplinary problems in a calmer and more loving way."

It's the old chicken/egg business. The teenager thinks: If only my parents weren't so dumb, up-tight and critical all the time, I might be able to talk to them. The parent thinks: If only he weren't so turned-off, sullen and resistant to every suggestion, I might be able to get in touch with him—he won't even give me a chance to express my affection.

Who can resolve the conundrum? Only the parents. They have to make an act of faith, by plunging into the child's defenses, the oftener the better. Usually the child cannot initiate behavior which might improve the relationship. He's far too shaky. We have all forgotten how awkward it was to move through the many stages from child to man or woman. Everything went wrong; we were all daily victims of mental, social, and physical lapses. The world noticed some of them, but *we* saw them all—perhaps more than were actually there. We hated ourselves for our failures. The word *jerk* was the mantra of my teenage interior monologue, and I recited it with a savage loathing. Who can tell a teen that he or she is *not* a jerk? That he is a competent human being, and lovable in the fullest sense? That his feelings and actions and physical looks are normal for his time in life, and that his problems are those that we have all known, and they are manageable? Who can tell a child that he is stronger than he thinks, and the world less hostile? And that his sins are not so heinous that they cannot be forgiven?

Only a parent.

Once the daily pattern of love and support is demonstrated the channels of communication are cleared. If, in a spirit of love, you ask your son to tell you about some of his friends, maybe he will also tell you how the side of the family car *really* got dented; and if you and your daughter have established a relaxed and confidential mood, perhaps she will reveal a little about the troubles at school and why she missed the deadline for her term paper. You don't have to give up your standards simply because you are acting out your feelings for your children. Create a moment of love first, and they may even listen as you explain the reasons why your principles are so important.

How do we express love? We do it first, as all animals do, by *touching each other*. We hug, kiss, cuddle; we caress, we stroke, we pet, and so on—and every touch has meaning. It expresses tenderness, concern, and reassurance. Novelist Ingrid Bengis, writing in *MS* magazine, records a scene in a small family restaurant in Italy:

"Sitting by myself in a corner, eating a five-course meal with wine, I again find my eye gravitating toward what I have just left. A father embraces his son, strokes his hair, kisses his mouth, holds him in his lap. A daughter scrambles up on a stool beside her father as he rings up a lunch bill on the cash register. There is a tenderness in the father's eyes which is so intimate, so natural, that I gasp inwardly with pleasure, conscious that the same gestures, in America, would seem glaringly conspicuous . . ."

Why is this so? Why does it take only a single generation for

Italian immigrants in this country to become as stoic, as afraid of touching, as any Anglo-Saxon? Is it because of the pioneer, frontier tradition, in which people had to focus all their energies on the physical—suppressing emotional display as a sign of weakness? Are we still watching too many old Gary Cooper movies on the "Late Show"? Or is it because we have become too automated, educated, and intellectualized—too buttoned-down emotionally, so that we can't get our souls wet with all that sloppy hugging and kissing? Most horrifying of all is the possibility that if we can't demonstrate affection, maybe we no longer know how to *feel*. We have allowed our society to dehumanize us.

The problem becomes critical in the early teen years. When Eric was twelve Marion and I used to marvel at his open and easy affectionate nature. Surely, we said, this is going to be a tremendous asset throughout his life. For exampl , every evening he would come to both his mother and me to say g od night, give us a kiss on the cheek, and present his own cheek in return. In just a few seconds we were able to communicate our love for each other and to receive emotional reserves for the coming night, and day.

Was it appropriate for me to be kissing a twelve-year-old son good night? How bloody Anglo-Saxon for the question even to occur to me! "He's a teenager in body," Marion said, "but one part of him hasn't got self-conscious yet. He comes to us at bedtime because this gesture serves a need, and it's all so sweet and natural that we ought to enjoy it while we can. It won't last long." She was right. Barely a month later Eric was not kissing anybody; in fact, he didn't even say good night any more. He just went to bed. What had happened—some big emotional storm? Not that we knew of. He wasn't angry at us especially; he had just become a teenager, and he was separating.

This didn't mean that he didn't need the kiss, and all it represented, as much as ever. But he suddenly had *seen* this gesture; it was childish to him and hence inappropriate. I was glad that *he* had made this observation and not me; nevertheless, the gulf had opened. At a time when he needed to feel our love in a physical sense more than ever, both sides were too embarrassed to find a way to do it. Every parent has gone through this. We are so eager to encourage the break-away, the feeling of independence and autonomy, that we don't want to insist on any pattern of behavior which a teen feels he has outgrown. Fathers and sons stare at each other helplessly across the dining-room table and pass carefully in the kitchen without ever touching. Mothers are timid too, even of their daughters, fearful of being shrugged off, as if to touch a teenager's body was to invade his or her privacy.

As a society we're stuck with the physical reserve which I suppose we inherited from the proper English along with their language; but as individual, thoughtful parents there is no reason we can't sneak in a little reassuring touching of our children. The more I thought about it the more annoyed with myself I became. Damn it, if I want to express my love to my son I can find some way to "touch" him. Perhaps bedtime was the right moment to experiment. That night I kept one wary eye on the late TV news and one eye on my son's room. When at last his light went off I knocked on his door. "Got enough covers?" I asked as I sat down on the bed.

You've got to put your hands someplace, I discovered, so it was natural for me to rest one hand gently on Eric's shoulder. Then as we made small talk, I found myself absentmindedly rubbing his back through the covers. Boy or girl, man or woman: everybody likes to have his back rubbed. "Good night, son," I said finally, letting my hand touch his cheek.

"Good night, Dad," he answered, in a tone which said that we had reestablished contact.

This interlude at the side of the bed doesn't have to last more than a minute or two, but because it's such a familiar pattern from the teenager's earlier years, it's not hard for him to drop his self-consciousness. I wish I could say that I visited each of my children every night, or that my wife had, but of course we didn't. We were busy or too tired to make the effort, or they were asleep before we knew it and the moment had passed.

The hardest time, of course, is right after you've had a fight with them. My wife and I would look at each other. "Well, she hates you less than me tonight," one of us would say. And so the Good Guy would go upstairs, knock hesitantly on the door, and hope not to be turned away. Sometimes we were but went in anyway, and sat down on the bed as usual. At this point you can't resume any aspect of the confrontation; you say something like: "Mom and I just want you to know that we love you very much." Then you kiss them, or make the usual tender gesture, and go. The message is that no matter how much we may disagree, even if we lose control and say things we don't mean, our basic feelings remain the same. They will never change.

Is it really necessary to remind them of this fact so often? Unfortunately, yes. To a teenager the supply of incoming trouble and pain seldom equals the available current supply of love and reassurance. For that matter, these elements are often out of balance for adults, too—that's one of the reasons we get married. Obviously the act of demonstrating love daily to our children can also help to stabilize our own lives.

It seems a bit shameful even to be articulating these things: they simply ought to *happen*. But they don't. We often have to look at the way we live and say, "That's not good enough." It struck me one day coming back from a business trip how glad I was to see my wife and children, and how eager each of them was to see me. I could hardly put my suitcase down before we were all hugging and kissing each other. Our culture had given us permission to display this feeling after a suitable absence. But the hell with "suitable," I thought; why do we have to wait? When I come home from the office now I feel that eight or ten hours away is long enough, and I give everybody a hug whether he or she is in the mood for it or not. *I'm* in the mood for it, and I have a right to tell them physically how I feel.

We all have a little more "Italian" in us than we think, if we will only give ourselves permission to let it out. When a teenager has had a great triumph in school or elsewhere it is not enough to say, in the stiff-upper-lip tradition, "Well done, son." There ought to be some whooping for joy, a whirling around, a heedless physical contact—at the very least an arm thrown across those broadening shoulders. The kids are right: we are buttoned-down. Let's unbutton, and act out our feelings. Yes, maybe it was never done that way when we were young—maybe our parents never taught us to express emotion in that way. But that's *our* problem; are we going to pass it on to them? Or are we going to break out and, embarrassed and awkward as we may feel sometimes, actually *show* our kids every day how much we love them, in a way they can't possibly mistake?

Most of us are good at non-physical attempts to reach out. I am forever cutting out newspaper articles and tearing out pages of magazines which I think will interest one of my children. I scribble notes at the top, making some point, and leave them at the breakfast table since none of us seems to be verbal in the morning. Marion frequently leaves loving notes on the kitchen blackboard if she isn't going to be there when the kids come home from school, but sometimes she does it even if she is in the house. Every family has many silent ways to express love and a feeling of belonging; but we can always do more.

Once when we were having an especially difficult time with Lisa I brought her home a different poster for her room for ten days in a row. All the posters said something about loving and caring or parent-child relationships. How much effort did this cost me? I picked them all out in one fifteen-minute session at a poster store and stuck them up on the walls of my office (my secretary thought I had flipped) until it was time to bring each one home. Yes, my daughter liked the posters and the messages, and this insignificant daily gift became a game of love which warmed us and helped us work through the problem. To tell the truth, I can't even remember what the problem was now, nor can Lisa. But we both remember the gesture.

These silent signs and symbols of caring are important, but once in a while we also need to make a flat-out verbal statement of *total approval.* I mean to lay it out blatantly in just so many words: You are my child, and I think you are the greatest! We really do feel

that way, don't we? Would we trade them for any other kids we
know? OK, then let's say it without shame. Everybody else is going
to qualify his admiration, restrain it out of a sense of decorum, if
nothing else. And, God knows, there are enough times when the
best *we* can muster is faint praise.

When our children are gone for a few days during the summer
or during other vacations, our troubles and their blemishes begin to
fade away. This may be the best time to pull out all the emotional
stops, because the need to express our love has accumulated. For
example, here is a letter I wrote to Eve at camp. I wanted to tell her
how much we totally approved of her as a daughter, and also to
reassure her about her physical appearance. Like many teens, she
was in a dither. Since she had recently shot up a couple of inches,
she thought she was going to be a giant. She worried about her
complexion although she hardly had a pimple. She thought her smile
was crooked, although the orthodontist had finally decided her teeth
were so normal he couldn't recommend treatment. Who can know
the agony of teen uncertainty? We all think we can recall those
times, but nobody remembers pain as it was. We have to assume
they are feeling more than we can see, and therefore no comfort we
can offer will ever be too much.

DEAR EVE,

I'm sorry your box of extra clothes and goodies hasn't arrived yet while all about you other people are receiving theirs.
Blame it on the U.S. mails. Mom actually went out and secretly
mailed your shipment two days *before* you left for camp, so that
this year it would turn up soon enough. By the time you read
this I hope you will be knee-deep in Butterfingers and chocolate
raisins, flashlight batteries, suntan lotion, and stamps.

We are much impressed with the lively letters you write,
full of information and vivid details. It's those sharp camera's
eye details which really make us understand what it is like to get
up at 6 A.M. before the others, to go out and feed Susie Q. We
can almost feel the communion between you and your horse in

the early morning stillness. That's good letter-writing, much better than I could ever manage at your age. And you know what else it is, Evie? It's generosity on your part, to make an effort to share your feelings with us. Parents are often grateful if kids deign to give them some kind of mechanical report on what they are doing, but what we really want to know is: how are you getting along on the inner level? We care about you so much that your unhappiness is ours and your joy is also ours.

One phrase at the end of your letter caught my eye. You closed with the words, "Your lovely daughter, Eve." Of course you were kidding, or thought you were, but maybe you weren't. We'd like to think you really believe it—that you are a lovely person in both looks and soul. Your Grandma Alice said that when she was your age (about 1910) people were always telling her, "Pretty Is as Pretty Does." That's true, obviously, but it begs the question that most young people really want to know: what does the world think of me? And, unfortunately, that usually means what does the world think of me at first glance?

Adolescents should feel more pleasure than pain, and when they don't it's usually because of foolish worries over things which either aren't so, or don't matter. When I was your age Jack, my best high-school buddy, and I spent a lot of time looking at noses in the mirror. We were convinced that our noses were so deformed as to be repulsive to girls. I called him "Ski" and he called me "Hook."

As you know, not long ago I went out to Detroit to visit him and we spent a marvelous three days together. One night I asked him how he felt about his nose now. "I haven't thought about it in years," he replied with some wonder. It was the same for me. Both noses, as it turned out, fell well within the normal range of facial adornment, and as we grew up it finally dawned on us that nobody had ever noticed them.

Similarly, as a girl your mother agonized over herself as some kind of female grotesque, simply because one year she shot up to her present height of 5'7½". The only boys she could look up to in high school were the basketball players, and they seemed chiefly enthralled by those little doll-like cheerleaders. Only Mom can tell you how much misery she experienced in this period, but in a few years the problem faded away for her, too. The boys suddenly had their accelerated growth period, and as an adult she found lots of men who never gave her height a second thought.

Dear daughter, do you see my point? Despite my reassurances I suppose you have some secret doubts about your person as you stare into your mirror there at camp. But honestly none of it matters, even if true. If you don't mention it to your friends they will never notice, because they are too busy worrying about their own grievous "defects." The rule to remember is that other people will love you for your whole self, not any separate part, and in fact they will *look at* you as a whole.

What do I see when I stand at a distance? I see a beautiful young woman. Sometimes you literally take my breath away. Studying the photo on my desk in front of me now, I just can't imagine any other features that God might have given you which would make you more attractive. Does my saying this surprise you? Have your mother and I ever said right out that we liked your *looks* as well as everything else about you? Parents make mistakes like that sometimes. Maybe we have been so busy praising you for your talents and achievements that we neglected to say that the real Essence of You is something superb. Mom and I can see it now, because we have been looking for a long time. In the proper time the world will notice, too. Be glad with yourself, daughter, and let all of us rejoice with you.

4 ✳

Opening the Adult Door

The concept of Adult at Eighteen does not mean that we say to our children: "Listen, kid, you see that raging sea over there? Well, you'd better learn to swim because on your eighteenth birthday we're going to throw you in."

Rather, we say to them, in many different ways: "I *know* you are going to be able to swim, because you and I are going to wade into the water together right now. This year you're going to learn to float, and if you sink just two inches my arms are going to be right under you so you don't get more than a mouthful of water. Next year you'll learn the crawl; you'll be going out over your head, but I'll be swimming right alongside. As soon as you can make a hundred yards by yourself, Mom and I won't be in the water with you any longer; we'll be sitting over there on that rock watching in case you get a cramp or something. Every year you'll practice swimming farther from the shore, until on your eighteenth birthday you feel confident about entering the long-distance race. Mom and I will be riding along in the launch now, cheering you as you go. You may or may not win the race, but none of us will be worrying about your ability to swim the distance."

How do we stay close enough to the child all through his teen years to know *exactly* how much support he needs? The almost daily attempt to reach out with a gesture of love, by both parents, pays double dividends. It gives the child (and the parents) strength, and it offers the child a chance to reveal his fears. Often mom and dad are the last people to know what a teen is really worrying about; he covers up because we are so constantly critical and so insistent upon his responding in a strong way when he just *can't*.

The interflow of love will give us some clues, but we also need more specific information about what is going on. We need to enter our kids' lives to a certain extent, and we have to bring them part way into our adult world. And, lord, none of this is easy! Husband, wife, daughter, son: all of us lead our own preoccupied existence and, unless we make a determined effort, these lives are not going to intersect much. It is possible for adults and teenagers to inhabit the same house and not really talk to each other for days, weeks, even months, except for conventionalized greetings as they happen to encounter one another in motion to or from some private activity.

As our children moved into their teen years, Marion and I began to feel a little desperate about this. We decided that we had to get in touch with each other as family members at least once during the day. But when? Mealtime seemed the only answer. Breakfast was out—we aren't "morning" people. So that meant supper. And that meant a problem for me.

I was running a high-pressure business at that time, had to do some business entertaining, and faced a fairly arduous commute both ways. My wife laid it on the line. "Look," she said, "I try to hold off dinner as late as I can; I know how hard it is for you to get home at any specific time, and I'm sympathetic to what you are trying to do in your work. But let's not fool ourselves. Either you find a way to get home most nights, or you're a weekend father like so many of the other men we know. Maybe you can catch the kids then and make up for the contact you missed. But weekends are busy, too; we all like to have some time off for fun and to please ourselves. You want to play golf, for example, and I don't blame you. What are we going to do?"

I didn't give her an answer for a while. We'll muddle through somehow, I thought. Except that if you have in the back of your mind that you want your kids to be Adult at Eighteen, you don't have too much time to muddle. Either you let them drift, without the essential insights needed for some kind of controlled development, or you accept the necessary priorities in business vs. family. What *is* most important after all? If you coin all the money in the world and lose your kids in the process, does that make you a great Success? If you're so good at the office, how come you can't organize your work life so that the business still moves ahead even if you find a little time for your family?

Most fathers go through this kind of internal debate and resolve the conflict. *They resolve it again and again.* The trouble is: you make a tremendous effort to compress the business day, to cut things off early enough to get home, and then when you finally get there, nothing happens. You raced home in time for dinner, you dragooned the kids to sit down face to face across the table, and *you can't get a word out of them.* You sit in baffled rage and ask yourself, what's the point of all this? There isn't any way we can talk to each other. And so tomorrow it's a little easier to let the pressures of the job take over; the workdays can easily provide more tangible psychological rewards than a sullen teenager at home.

My son unexpectedly showed me one way to begin. It was the usual weekday dinner. "What's new in school?" I'd asked. One by one, my three offspring furnished the monosyllabic negatives every parent knows so well. Nothing had happened in school that day. Nothing had happened after school. Apparently nobody had any plans for anything to happen that evening, or even the next day. It was a complete stonewall of glum teenage faces, and my flashpoint arrived.

"Listen!" I shouted. "We're going to have a new rule around here. When I ask you about your day you're going to tell me *one thing*, good or bad—you decide."

After a stunned moment Eric looked up over his uneaten green beans and said coolly: "Why should we? You never tell us anything about what you do."

Right between the eyes. *That's not true*, I was about to protest.

But on the other hand he didn't usually answer me in that tone; he sounded as though he believed it. Maybe *I* hadn't been communicating very well, either. Could that possibly be? My second thought was: I didn't know you *cared*. (Breathes there a father so free of self-pity that he doesn't feel his years of sweat are taken for granted by both kids and wife?)

"All right," I sighed wearily. It had been a tough day at the office, full of crises and people who thought they were misunderstood. The last thing I wanted at that moment was to rehash it, but somehow I managed to dredge up an anecdote that I thought might vaguely amuse them. To my surprise, the kids thought it was funnier than I did, and along with my wife they asked a dozen questions. Then, one by one, it was their turn to report. I began to understand that it was an *effort* for them, too, to select and verbalize an experience which could interest the whole family. Like me, they had to do some preliminary explaining so we could understand the point of the story; like me, they didn't feel like reliving the day's experience, especially if it hadn't been triumphant. But clearly all the members of the family *had* to make the effort that night, and when we were through we had talked quite a while, and each of us was rather pleased with himself.

Was this a "breakthrough" which solved our family communications problems? Of course not. The next night it was the same thing all over again.

Even so, Marion and I had learned something; from then on we took the lead in opening up our own daily experiences as we sat down at the dinner table, and this gave us a certain moral right to insist that the kids make the same kind of effort. No, during the early teens it never did flow easily, but gradually, gradually the message began to penetrate: if you want to belong to a family you have to let the family into your life just a little.

We also found another useful benefit in the dinner talk—our kids began to think of us as fellow human beings. At certain periods parents aren't really people—they are institutions of authority. (One evening watching the kids drift through the house absorbed in themselves, I got the eerie feeling that they saw us as something like those dour statues on Easter Island, thirty-foot-tall granite heads, mysterious, powerful, but essentially unknowable. Symbols for the natives to fear and carefully walk around.)

Now, slowly, as Marion and I revealed ourselves, the "statues" began to melt into recognizable humans struggling, just like the kids, to get through their day. In time my kids started to understand why I went on business trips, where I went, and whom I saw. They began to learn the cast of characters at the office, not because they wanted to but simply because the names came up again and again; thus the kids discovered how my fellow workers fitted into the mechanism that was our business. When they came in to visit me occasionally, the tour of the offices did not produce a turned-off mask of teen politeness; my children wanted to put the names, faces, and job functions together. The real world of adults had opened up to them a little; and they found that they weren't turned off by it.

When my kids bring home their friends from high school and college I sometimes ask them what their fathers do. They reply with a perfunctory occupational label, of course, but then I say: "Yes, but what exactly does he do in that job?" It's a rare kid these days who really knows. And if he doesn't know, how can he be interested? A father, through sheer inertia or pride or something, has cut his children off from any participation in the most vital part of his life, his work. And he has cut them off from learning what that work means—both to him and to them. They can't see him as a working human being unless he lets them, and in fact unless he *requires* them to look at him in this way.

The reason teenagers find everything so "irrelevant" is that they aren't forced to participate in, or even to look at, the triumphs and defeats of ordinary adult life. How many fathers take wife *and* kids out to celebrate when they get a raise? How many fathers let their kids know that they are so unhappy with their present job that they are actively looking for another position? Why not? No parent wants to worry his children, but what better way can he teach them about life than to let them see it being played out in front of them? Sometimes the cup overflows with triumph and sometimes things are just plain *tough*. Any father whose self-esteem requires him to present a façade of eternal calm success deserves to be thought of as an Easter Island head.

And the same thing for Mother. As the children move into the teen years at last, requiring less absolute custodial care, a woman finally has the time to think more about her private life and her role outside the family. If she hasn't been working all along, she may resume her career, or begin a new one, or she may choose to focus her energies in some other way on an activity which interests or concerns her. Why should the children not know all about this, and in fact play a major supporting role in the effort? An important milestone on the road to self-knowledge is reached when a teen discovers that his mother no longer has the time to wait on him *because now she has something more important to do.*

He isn't going to know that her new vital activity is important unless she tells him that it is. He has to see how excited and involved she is with her new work before he can psychologically agree that it is *fair* for her to stop performing as his private servant. If father confirms his wife's new role as important, she also begins to assume a stronger image in the eyes of the children. Just about the time they'd begun to dismiss her as "old mom," the housemaid who isn't quite hip to the real world, she suddenly starts doing something new and rather difficult outside the home. Parental respect is enhanced not only by allowing our children to see that we are engaged in a significant activity, but in demanding that they cooperate so that adult goals can be achieved.

And so at the dinner table Marion began to involve us in her plans. She had no desire to return to her former career in commercial art; rather she was going to do serious painting and sculpture, seriously. No more grabbing an hour here and there between household chores, with the easel set up in the basement; she and a friend were going to rent a skylit studio over a garage a few blocks away. She simply wouldn't be available at home for five or six hours every day.

Of course it wasn't easy, and she told us about her problems as she went along. We talked about the nature of creativity as well as the psychological problems an artist faces, and slowly the house filled up with paintings, sculpture, and assemblages of various kinds. We liked some of them, and didn't understand some, but we were proud that she'd done them. Finally the day came when she had her first show at a commercial gallery, and she was written up in the paper. The kids were there on the crowded opening night, pouring champagne, a little awed at what Mom had wrought. Here was cause and effect: several years of daily struggle, of starting over and trying new ideas, new materials, new forms; several years of dry spells and discouragement but persistent effort. They had seen it all, and now here was the payoff—a crowd of people looking at and admiring their mother's work.

"But You Aren't My Teacher!"

Of course this "opening up" by each member of the family about his or her activities of the day is only the starting point. As important as it is to be able to penetrate each other's lives to a certain extent, parents and children also need a wider arena for conversation beyond the specific and personal. *They need to talk about the whole adult world.* Kids need to understand there *is* a world out there beyond the family cocoon, and that it's both tremendously exciting and horrendously disturbing (not to mention changing faster than ever before in history). Parents have an obligation to tell their children not only what's happening, but how to think about it.

Back in the mid-nineteenth century we had a political faction called the "Know Nothing" Party. The largest group of Know Nothings of our time, however, is our teenagers. The most cataclysmic political, economic, and social changes are simply non-events to many teens. If an earthquake doesn't shake them personally it hasn't happened, nor do they want to know about it. The mass media spew out millions of words and pictures; they are ignored. The schools are very good at pouring information over a child's head, but unless someone has first persuaded him that, yes, this *is* relevant to you, he's not going to let much of this soak in, either. How do they get this way—our half-grown children floating around in the fourth dimension, here but not really here?

Again, it begins in the home. If the children have never heard their parents talk about ideas and issues and what's going on in the world, why should they suddenly see any reason to be involved when they become teens? Like most parents, Marion and I had always assumed that we were explaining the world to our children as they grew up, but slowly it dawned on us that most of our intellectual talk was not in the presence of the kids—it was privately with each other. The whole family never got together long enough at any one time to explore the world of ideas.

When Lisa was sixteen I decided we'd make at least one small organized experiment in this direction. Every Thursday night each member of the family would bring one or more newspaper or magazine articles to the table, and after we'd had dessert we'd spend an hour talking about them. Mainly this was for the benefit of Lisa, but even though Eric was only eleven and Eve ten, why should they not participate too? Yes, some of the information might be too complex, but the *attitudes* we expressed toward it would not be.

Lisa said a Current Events Night might be fun, but the younger children thought it was a terrible idea. "Why, that's just like school!" Eve protested. "You're not my teacher." *Not her teacher?* Good God, is everything split apart for a child today? Specialists for every separate function of the body, mind, and soul—and never anybody to bring it all together? Surely if anybody can and should be a general practitioner, it is a parent. "Eve," I said, "Mother and I are your real teachers about everything in life. At school you will have dozens of instructors in your educational career, but they really work for us. It is our taxes which pay for them and our decision, indirectly, what they should teach. Right now it is our direct obligation and privilege to show you the *meaning* of what they are teaching, and we plan to do that in every sphere of your life until you are eighteen."

Well, there was great grumbling and mumbling, but on Thursday night everybody had an article. I have no memory of what subjects were discussed that first night, but several months later I did make some notes on one of our family "news article" discussions:

Eric, the airplane fanatic, led off the evening with a newspaper clipping about the resumption of the B-52 bombings in Vietnam. He had some impressive figures on the total tonnage of bombs dropped on that poor country—how many times more than all of World War II. This led to a general discussion of President Nixon's policy, and we reviewed once more the bad side and the good side of Communism as it affected the liberty and the welfare of individuals. Would it be a good idea in this country? Was it right for Vietnam? And if not, how many more people should we drop bombs on to stop it? Eric, as usual, was the impatient hard-liner—if the enemy won't give up, use the A-bomb, he said. Lisa and Eve were in favor of letting the Vietnamese vote on it, but Marion pointed out how difficult it is to get an honest election on this subject.

Lisa read a report on the rise of food prices in the United States, and we analyzed what inflation had done to our income and to that of poor people. I said that before she was born I had made a five-dollar bet with a friend that Lisa would be a girl, and I'd put that money in a bank account for her. We discussed what the five dollars would have bought sixteen years ago and what it would buy now.

Marion displayed a newspaper map which showed the population distribution in our county by race, and how it had changed in the last ten years. We discussed the reasons why blacks wanted to move out of the centers of big cities but why there were so few of them living in our neighborhood. We decided that if some blacks looked at a house on our block we would go out of our way to be friendly to them.

For my article, I brought us all up to date on the Presidential primaries and the candidates, upon whom we seriously disagreed. Marion suggested it was possible to bicycle down to the headquarters of two of the candidates to get some of their literature and campaign buttons.

When Eve's turn came, she showed us a photo of an albino giraffe born in the Tokyo zoo. Lisa groaned, "Oh, you baby, animals aren't news." Eve vigorously disputed this, but then produced a second article (which she read with some difficulty) about a Senate subcommittee bill to liberalize Social Security. "I think we should take better care of old people," Eve concluded. When we had recovered from our astonishment, we discussed what Social Security was in this country and how, although we have the highest standard of living in the world, other societies *do* make better provision for their old and needy. We also discussed the increase in taxes which would be needed to provide similar benefits.

I'm sure I took these notes because it was one of our better sessions. The discussion actually ran about an hour and a half, and we were all so excited and involved that we never noticed the time. Obviously the discussion of any one of the major issues (Communism, inflation, racism) was oversimplified, even superficial, to accommodate all age levels. But every parent knows you can't overdose these things; you use an eyedropper—one drop every day for five thousand days—and suddenly the child *knows*, without understanding how this came to be.

Of course reading the newspapers and magazines for an article was a "drag," and so, no matter how successful the previous session, every week started back at point zero with childish complaints (Lisa included) about having to do this special kind of "homework." We persisted stubbornly for two and a half years until Lisa left for college; then the parental flesh grew weak. You know how those things go—sheer lack of feedback convinces you that it just isn't worth the effort to keep pushing.

"What?" Lisa cried when she came home on college vacation, "you've given up the news articles? You *can't*. I always thought it was terrific that we talked about things like that in the family."

Truly? Marion and I inquired. Had she really learned anything from all those sessions? "How would I know?" Lisa answered. "Kids never know when they learn anything. But I never had any doubt how you felt about politics and foreign affairs and stuff—and I suppose I got a lot out of just listening to the way your thought processes worked. Anyway, you certainly gave me the message that we were part of the world."

5 ❄

Lessons of the Paper Route

The damnable frustration of raising kids is that you never can tell if you are doing things right. *Everything* has to be taken on faith; if your common sense says that a certain parental position has got to make your child more independent and responsible and happier with himself, then you go ahead and do it. But most of the time you feel you are stumbling forward in the dark, arms outstretched, bumping up against obstacles, turning this way and that, as you grope for any ray of daylight.

Mostly all we have is negative evidence. If our kids aren't in trouble, if they are functioning at all in school, if they have a few friends, if they volunteer to talk with us once in a while: well, things could be worse. But if we are committed to a program of full maturity at eighteen, we need something better than this. We need enough positive evidence to keep up our own morale, to give us the psychological courage to go on making constant demands in a constructive way which does not damage our children's feelings that we love them.

Often something happens by pure accident and we see that a child has learned a lesson from it; then the same type of event occurs again with positive results. Soon the parents are arranging to have these lessons experienced in a more organized way; they become part

57

of the program. For example, let me give you one small pattern in Eric's early development: *

THE PROFESSIONAL CAR WASHER. Every family has two kinds of children: the savers and the spenders. Eve was our saver, Lisa ranked halfway between, and Eric was certainly the family consumer par excellence. His eye hardly lit on an object that he did not desire to possess. Fortunately, Eric was always willing to work for the money he needed, if somebody would only offer him a job.

One Saturday when he was about eleven he called me out to the driveway to see the family car which he had just washed. "How much are you going to pay me?" he asked. I looked it over and handed him a dollar. "Hey, you said you'd pay the same as the drive-in car wash," he protested.

"That's right," I replied. "There are two kinds of car washes: a Professional Job and a Little Boy Job. You've given me a Little Boy Job, and that's only worth half the price."

"What do you mean?" he cried in dismay.

"The windows are streaky, you forgot to vacuum the floor of the backseat, and you didn't wash the wheels at all. How come?" He shrugged. "Look," I went on, "you have a lot of respect for Joe Namath, and tomorrow he's going to be playing the best game he possibly can even though the Jets don't have a chance to make the playoffs. Win or lose he's going to be paid for his work, but he's still trying his damnedest because he has pride in what he's doing. A pro never stops giving everything he's got to it. If you are a Professional Car Washer, then do a professional job with some pride."

"Will you pay me the two dollars if I do?"

---

* I do not tell these personal anecdotes in any spirit of parental one-upmanship (how *discerning* the parents, how *responsive* the children). We have had as many failures with our children as most parents, I'm sure; but human nature mercifully allows us to forget them quickly. Anyway, parents don't want to read about other people's failures—they're discouraged enough as it is. The point of this book is that Adult at Eighteen *can* work, as impossibly immature as your children or mine may seem at any one moment.

"Gladly."

Well, the second time around he *did* do a Professional Job—better than the commercial car wash, in fact. And from then on, with one or two exceptions, he always did a Professional Job. There was no halfway position—no compromise. Did this mean that from then on he tackled all his other household jobs and other endeavors with "professional" pride, and the "little boy" vanished? No, Eric had merely learned the lesson *in regard to car washing*. As every parent and teacher knows, the lesson has to be learned over and over again in individual transactions. It's as if a child keeps each experience locked away in a separate room in his mind; with luck something happens in his late teens which allows him to open a window into these various rooms, and if he finds the same evidence in a number of them he is at last able to draw a general conclusion. If we want our children to work through the basics of adulthood by the time they are eighteen, we have to be looking for patterns of similar positive experience to fill up those "rooms."

THE LAWN KING. The next major example in our household occurred a year later. Our lawn had gone into a mysterious decline, and so, like many of our neighbors, we decided to hire one of the new franchised commercial lawn services to build it up. Eric, who by this time was sharing lawn-mowing duties with Lisa, complained about the lawn service from the start. The men were in too much of a hurry and didn't care enough, it seemed to him; and finally one day he casually declared, "I could do a better job than they do."

Marion and I opened our mouths at the same instant. "Why *don't* you take over?" we asked. "We'll be happy to pay you the same amount we give the lawn service if you think you can do a Professional Job." This involved considerable study on his part as to how much seed was called for, and what kind of grass we wanted to grow. And what kinds of fertilizer we needed, and when the various weed-killers and bug-slayers had to be applied. He got so wrapped up in giving our lawn the very best of everything, in fact, that we had to hold him down on his purchases, for fear he wouldn't end up with a little profit for his labor.

He made a few mistakes, of course. In the fall he delayed for two months raking up a pile of leaves, and this destroyed a small patch of grass. On the front lawn he spilled a bag of fertilizer, and this burned another hole. But in the spring he planted seed and watered carefully, and in the end we had such a terrific lawn that we bought an old-fashioned croquet set. Best of all, the days of nagging kids about lawn mowing were over. Eric took over full responsibility for all aspects of lawn care as part of the package: all the money went to him, all the praise, and all the pride. And he *was* proud. On a summer evening he liked sprinkling with the hose, just like the other householders on our street; and early one Sunday morning I saw him walking around his lawn still in his pajamas, looking for weeds and feeling his grass with his bare feet.

PAINS OF A PAPER BOY. Of course there was a limit to the number of jobs at home we were willing to pay Eric for. He lived in this house too; he had a responsibility to contribute some labor just like the rest of us. But what can I do to earn more money? he complained. We made numerous suggestions, most of which he vetoed. Once in a burst of energy he hand-lettered two dozen file cards offering his services to shovel snow, take care of lawns, or do other handyman jobs; but then he found himself unable to go around ringing doorbells to present his offer. We didn't insist—it *is* hard to learn to sell yourself to strangers, and there would be time enough for this later.

And so, at the age of fourteen, he began to think about a morning paper route. The money astonished me; he would be able to earn at least twenty dollars a week, including tips. Apparently it's a sign of our times that even this princely wage cannot induce the average American boy to get up in the morning seven days a week in all weather, and so grown men often moonlight before their regular jobs by taking two or three paper routes and tossing the papers on customers' lawns as they drive by in their cars.

I'd had a morning route myself in high school, so I thought I ought to give Eric the bad news before he committed himself:

"1. It's sheer hell to drag yourself out of bed early every morning seven days a week without a letup. I had to get up at five A.M., but you're lucky—they deliver the papers right to your door, so you can sleep until six.* But you have to understand that Mom and I are *never* going to wake you up. It's your job and you have your own alarm.

"2. You're never going to be able to stay awake in school unless you have the self-discipline to go to bed. You have to decide that you can never start a 10 P.M. TV show, no matter how attractive it is. You have to sacrifice the temporary pleasure of the TV show for the larger satisfaction of having a job which fills your other needs in life. Most kids can't do this, son; they are too childish to give up immediate gratifications even though they would dearly love to make twenty dollars a week like you.

"3. We want you to believe in your power to do a job without help from anyone, just as a grown man does. So don't ever ask us to drive you around in the car. No matter how bad the weather gets, you can make it on your bicycle.

"4. We're not quitters in this family. If you take this job, knowing what I've just said, you've got to stick with it for at least six months, or until you find some other regular job which will satisfy your personal needs. Is that agreed? If you tell the man you're going to take this route, you're not going to quit on him like the other kids have."

Eric blithely assured me he could see no problem. But that first Monday in January produced the worst weather of the year. We heard his alarm go off, and about 6:30 we came down to find Eric with his papers all folded. He was staring out into a blizzard. Four inches of snow had fallen during the night, and the wind was swirling gusts up to forty miles an hour. "I can't go out there," he said.

"Yes you can."

* Oh, we had it *tough* in the old days. I hate myself when I make these comparisons. But what parent can resist?

"I can't ride my bike."

"They're plowing the streets now."

"You aren't going to take me?"

"I told you never to ask."

With a black stare of anger and despair he plunged out the door and promptly fell down the front steps. His papers spilled into the snow, and the list of his customers blew out of his hand. The last we saw of him, as we closed the door, was a pathetic figure floundering across the lawn after the precious list of names and addresses.

"Oh, you heartless beast," my wife said, putting her arm around me.

"God, you're right," I answered. I waited for her to suggest that we get out the car, and she waited for me, and neither of us said it. By the time he had finished the route Eric was already late for school, but he had discovered that it is possible to deliver papers in the snow. By the second day he had learned the route well enough so he wasn't late. By the third day he actually had time for breakfast. Then another blizzard hit him, worse than the first.

Everybody in the family still remembers the first week of the paper route. But Eric didn't quit, and slowly he grew rather proud of this fact. He had other lessons to learn, of course:

❊ The newspaper had sagely supplied him with a Xeroxed sheet to distribute to his customers, identifying Eric as the new deliveryman and giving his home telephone number. It took him several weeks of telephoned complaints before he delivered his product to each customer so that (a) it could be found in the snow, and (b) it would be in something better than soaking-wet condition.

❊ Collecting was a problem. If a customer wasn't home Eric seldom went back again until the next week. Consequently he was always behind, and sometimes on Saturday didn't even have enough cash to pay for the week's papers. For a while we advanced him what he needed, but then we stopped playing banker. He had to meet his bills on time like any businessman.

❊ He was astonishingly good about going to bed and getting up on time, but in February he had a week's school vacation. I found him still asleep at 8:15 A.M. "It's vacation!" he protested wearily, as if I were being totally unreasonable. This was such archetypical teen thinking that I couldn't be angry. Gently, I explained that the world did not function on Eric's schedule; the world was not on vacation that week. His customers still wanted to read their morning paper in the morning.

Gradually, as his service improved, his customers began to compliment him, and they increased their tips. One man gave him a dollar extra every week to get off his bike and put the paper in his mailbox; another man gave him a baseball. By spring two families had hired him to do lawnwork. It took a fourteen-year-old boy three months to master all the lessons this simple job had to teach, and they were considerable, when you stop to think about them.

6 ❄

Give Up the Power—
Before They Take It

Teen: You treat me like a *kid* . . . You don't really trust me.

Parent: If I treat you like a kid it's because you *act* like one.

We've all been through this rondelet of accusation, each side feeling that it is only reacting to the unprovoked aggression of the other. Can't *somebody* break out of this vicious circle? Yes, a parent can swallow hard and respond in a different way:

Parent: I apologize if I've been doing that. I really want to change my attitude—I want very much to treat you fairly.

If we can say this and mean it, we have instantly defused the emotion and the contest of wills between us. We can now talk in a friendly way about the real problems and, better yet, the teenager has been challenged to make a similar act of generosity—to try to see the issues from our point of view so that he can also treat us "fairly."

As a nation we have been slow to realize that our enormous power can only be deployed in a very limited way in compelling other people to act as we think best. It's the same with parents. Sometimes we have to suffer a major defeat before the idea sinks in. If the Imperial President has vanished, so too has the Imperial Father (and the Queen Mother), in favor of a guy the common people trust, and can talk to.

That's why Adult at Eighteen offers immediate help to parents. It forces us to examine—perhaps for the first time—the nature of the power we exercise over our children. For many years we have been dictating every detail of their lives, and we have fallen into the automatic assumption that We Know Best. It is very *efficient* to order our kids' lives. It saves time and it saves mistakes, and anyway we are suffused with a warm glow of virtue because it's all for Their Benefit.

But our kids are growing up, and they see it differently. Every human being has a strong drive to discover the meaning of Self. He has to find out who he is—and he senses that he can't do this as long as his parents are painting the picture for him. If parents are unyielding, a young man or woman often feels compelled to strike out wildly in a gesture of independence, even though the action may be self-destructive. Parents react sharply "to get things under control," and thus the battle is joined.

It seems to me that the key to living with a teenager is to avoid letting him build up a frustrated head of steam. When we suggest by our actions (if not by our words) that "as long as you live in my house and eat my bread you'll do things my way," we are, in effect, sentencing him to a penal term. It looks like *years* before he'll be free, and he can't wait that long. He attempts to escape, in both overt and subtle ways, and we all end up feeling unappreciated, angry, and slightly desperate.

What can we do? Accept the fact that it is better for us to give away part of our power when it will be received with gratitude than it is to push our teens into the position where they will take power from us by force. Mies van der Rohe popularized the concept of "Less Is More" in his architecture, and the same idea applies to parental control of maturing children. The more we try to govern by fiat the less effect we have.

No matter what our views on raising kids, it is hard to deny that we have to find ways to communicate. If we go to a counselor for help in family matters, he or she is almost sure to propose some kind

of family conference which deals openly with power stereotypes.*

Here is how a conference is handled in our family during the
second and third teen years:

Marion and I begin by restating the goals of Adult at Eighteen
and compliment the kids in specific areas in which they have handled
themselves well. We express our love and our satisfaction with the
progress they are making. Then we ask for a critique of our own
performance. Have we as parents really done what we said we
would do at the last meeting? Have we attempted to treat them as
adults? Have we extended trust? Have we respected their privacy,
spoken to them courteously, cut down on the nagging, and generally
acted in a loving and supportive way?

If there is no immediate response we wait, and slowly the de-
murs come out. We ask for specific instances of our failure, and we
try not to argue these matters—even if they seem unfair or unrealistic. If we simply can't approve a suggested course of action we
always try to present a counter-offer rather than a flat veto, or at
least to fix a date on which we will again consider the idea.

At this point we have (a) described our pleasure in having them
as children, (b) praised them for achievements, (c) encouraged them
to express the resentments they feel toward us, (d) shown them that
we sincerely want to solve any problems, and (e) proved that we
frequently are prepared to change our views and our conduct, rather
than requiring the kids to do all the adapting.

Then it is our turn to point out some very specific areas in
which we feel things are not working. Since most parents can get up
a nearly endless list, it is important to agree with your spouse ahead
of time just which issues should be brought up—and how they can
be presented in a way likely to trigger constructive discussion. No
point should be pressed when it becomes emotional, nor should the
parental recital of complaints overshadow that of the kids. The con-

* For a good book with explicit instructions and transcripts of actual family
discussions see *Family Council*, by Dr. Rudolf Dreikurs, Shirley Gould, and Dr.
Raymond J. Corsini (Chicago: Henry Regnery, 1974).

ference should end with a repetition of how satisfied we are at the progress that has been made.

One of the most critical aspects of the power relationship is the teen's feeling that he is free to leave the house. It's not enough for him to know that we can no longer physically stop him from going; he has to leave with our blessing, and without the burden of our fears.

We have never fixed a "curfew" for any of our kids. Before they went out at night we expected them to volunteer some information about their destination and who would be with them. When they asked, "What time do I have to be home?" we would respond, "Well, what time seems reasonable to you?" It was understood that if they failed to arrive home shortly after the agreed-upon time it would be regarded as a major breach of faith. A few months before her eighteenth birthday Lisa was saying she didn't know when she would be home, and we had so much confidence in her that we didn't worry.

Physical liberty to come and go is so important to developing teens that we simply have to let them write their own rules, within reason. It helps if you like and respect their friends, and this is only possible if your children feel comfortable in bringing friends home fairly often, so that you can come to know them.

We also have regular sessions with our kids in which we lay out all our fears, and ask them to help develop defensive strategies. All too often parents never make it clear *exactly* what it is they are worrying about or develop all the reasons why the fear is real. Sometimes the kids can convince us that our information is inaccurate or out-of-date, or the conclusions we draw are exaggerated. But just as often when we cite our current sources and our past experience in a given matter, we can persuade them that the problem is serious and worth their attention. If we then encourage them to devise their own solutions, we feel much more confident when they leave the house—day or night.

For example, if a girl knows about a series of rapes in the town recently and is approached by a stranger on a dark street, what should she do? Maybe she shouldn't have been there in the first place, the kids said; maybe she should have arranged some transportation or at least found friends to accompany her. But in any case she should walk faster and, if pursued, she can *run*—straight up on the nearest porch and ring a doorbell for help. We felt confident that Lisa and Eve would not be too timid to take this action while the "situation" was still developing.

If a boy is getting off a bus in New York City alone for the very first time in his life, heading for Yankee Stadium, how can he avoid being mugged by a teen gang? Dress inconspicuously, keep your mouth shut, and avoid flaunting money, Eric said. And be aware of what's going on around you, we added. To be "street-wise" is to watch whoever's watching you, and to move on quickly if it looks like trouble.

These days it's possible that each of our teens is going to find himself at a party or other social gathering which is turning on with hard drugs. He or she may feel pressure to go along, including some taunts from good friends. What attitude should he take? "Make some excuse and get out of there," is the solution my kids give. Is this just a glib answer to pacify parental fears? The reply came so spontaneously and with such conviction that I believe them. Yes, we are certainly going to discuss the drug problem again and again, but Marion and I are no longer frightened by it. And I think our kids are proud that we aren't.

Psychotherapist Shirley Gould writes, "People respond to life as *they* believe it to be, not necessarily to things as they are or appear to others. Each person—child and adult—has an individual perception of the world and the people within it. That perception is absolutely unique; no one else has that particular set of views and thoughts, and no one else can accurately know how it is and what it looks like. . . . People have choices and make choices but not in complete freedom. One can act only within the possibilities and within the situation he or she perceives." *

* In *Teenagers: The Continuing Challenge* (New York: Hawthorn Books, 1977).

As parents we often subconsciously believe that our children fail to act in the way we would like simply because they are immature. If we are wise, however, we will proceed very tactfully to discover just what their perceptions are before we jump to the conclusion that they are acting inappropriately.

For example, a neighbor of ours was surprised while driving to work one Monday morning to see her son George and a close friend walking about a mile from their high school classes—and heading in the wrong direction. She drove on without stopping and George apparently did not see her. That night at dinner the conversation went like this:

MOTHER: Have a good day today?

GEORGE: Ummm, I guess so.

FATHER: Anything unusual happen?

GEORGE (*suddenly cautious*): No . . .

MOTHER: Well, a funny thing happened to me this morning about 8:30. I spotted you and your friend Mike walking down North Park Street, and you looked like you had some definite place in mind you were headed for.

GEORGE: Oh?

As it turned out, a new electronics store was staging a grand opening that morning at a nearby shopping center, and had advertised an important piece of radio equipment at a third off to the first twenty buyers. George, who at age fifteen was already the family wizard in things mechanical and electrical, was at that time involved in building his own ham radio station. He had the money for this new equipment and, along with his friend, wasn't about to miss this early-bird bargain. The two boys had then returned to George's house to assemble and test the equipment; the next thing they knew it was noon and there didn't seem to be much point in going to school so late.

Please note that in listening to this conversation both mother and father resisted the temptation to trap their son by forcing him to say he'd gone to school that day. The mother simply brought the situation out into the open in a calm way before George was tempted to lie. Many parents feel they are in an adversary position with their teens, and if they don't jump at an opportunity to get one-up they will never make their kids listen—or obey. But nobody can be friends with somebody who is trying to trap him, even if he suspects that he is in the wrong.

The parents here tried to see the situation through George's eyes. Given his passion for electronics, they had to agree that this was an important, and rather rare, opportunity to buy the needed equipment at a discount. Perhaps, though, George might have then gone on to school to make his ten o'clock class—and tested the new purchase *after* school?

This led to a general discussion of what school is all about and the importance of structured, formal study in addition to the scientific investigations that one might make on his own. Since his parents were being so reasonable, George had to agree that both were necessary. In fact, it came out that he had never skipped school before and had no present plans to do so again. Without quite realizing it, George at this point had been led to make a decision for himself about cutting classes without a good reason, and he had made a kind of promise to his parents. But it hadn't been extorted—he'd volunteered it.

That was the end of the discussion. The mother and father now knew something more about their son's attitude toward school, and had one more reason to believe generally that George was not likely to make decisions which were seriously self-destructive.

But if he felt his parents were all *that* understanding, couldn't George have told them at the breakfast table what he planned to do? No, that's asking too much. Nobody who is approaching adulthood wants to explain every move he makes—in effect to ask for permission. If he thinks it's right and reasonable—if he's determined to do it anyway—why get into a hassle that may not prove necessary if he just keeps his mouth shut?

That's the way we adults work, isn't it? If we expect more from our teens, maybe we haven't *really* decided to treat them as grownups.

7 ❊

The Children's Phone,
or How the Israelis and Arabs
First Learned to Co-Exist

Very hesitantly I reveal to you that our two younger kids, since their early teens, have had their own private telephone. Yes, that's right, not just a phone extension, but their own line out of the house, with instruments in each of their rooms and their own telephone number. Can you believe this indulgence? After all I've said?

The reason I never tell friends about this is that it requires too much explaining; but in fact the children's phone proved to be an excellent solution to several problems in our family.

"It seems rather marvelously unreal that Eric and Eve actually have gotten together to lobby for this thing," Marion said to me late one night. "I can't remember when they last spoke a civil word to each other."

"Me either," I replied.

If you have two teen kids close in age you know what we were talking about. Somewhere in this shining land there must be two siblings who love and respect each other all their lives, and who do not tease, harass, make fun of, contradict, and complain about each other, or battle over every word and gesture. Lisa, because she was at least five years older, always received quasi-adult respect, but Eric and Eve—only fifteen months apart—lived in their own quiet undeclared guerrilla war. Marion and I mediated and proselytized endlessly for a little mutual *courtesy* as a minimum standard of conduct; but like the UN we were seldom successful in arranging anything more than a few days' truce.

"They were up in Eve's room for an hour this afternoon conspiring about what they were going to say to us," Marion went on. "The last time he was in her room she threatened to kill him."

"All I know is that I tried to phone you three times to say I'd be late for dinner."

"That's because they were talking to the telephone company business office," Marion said. "I don't know how often they called that poor woman before they got all the facts straight. They even tried to put me on to talk with her once, but I refused."

I looked my wife right in the eye. "Maybe we ought to consider agreeing to this," I said.

"*What!*" she howled. "Their own telephone? I can't believe you're serious!"

"Bob Lackey called me at the office today and said he'd been trying every night for a week to get me for a golf game. He said if we put in a children's phone he'd pay for it. It was either that or carrier pigeons. And Lisa says she's getting discouraged trying to call home from college."

"Thank God we don't have *three* at home at the same time. Well, the kids will simply have to stop talking so much. They come in from school and call up the friends they've just left."

I sighed. "Yes, and they do their homework over the phone. But are we really going into the business of monitoring all their calls for time and content, like some Big Brother telephone operator?"

My wife groaned.

"Good God, we're trying to cut down the daily confrontations, aren't we?"

"Yes," Marion said. "So what are we going to do?"

"I don't know. What do other parents do?"

"They don't put in private telephone lines for their kids."

"Maybe their kids never offered to pay for them."

"Oh, *come on.*"

"I'm serious," I said. "Look how they presented their case. It wasn't just the usual infantile I-want-it-because-I-want-it demand. They didn't whine. They calmly said that it would solve all our phone-use problems, it wouldn't cost us a penny, and it would make them very happy. That's adult logic. They started out by telling us what it would do for us."

"They can't pay for a private phone."

"Well, I guess they can—if it's true the phone company offers a package deal with a second line for only $8.50 a month. Since they each get a dollar a week allowance they could share the cost and that would cover it."

"But that would take their whole allowance! What if they want a candy bar or something? They'd be begging me."

"You heard them. They're going to baby-sit or do yardwork for their spending money. I think I'm perfectly capable of refusing them any other spending money, aren't you? They really got to me when they threw my own words back. I said the purpose of an allowance was to teach them how to handle money. So they answered that if they wanted to cut out candy and ice cream in favor of the pleasure of having their own phone that should be their decision, not ours."

Marion had to smile. "What really got *me* is that they're not only talking to each other but they actually have worked out this whole plan together. It's so nice to have them acting humanly. If we give them a phone they'll be back at each other's throat worse than ever."

"No, they won't. If they don't act decently with each other we'll pull it out. We'll have a little leverage then."

"Big talk," Marion said. "You wouldn't do it."

"Hell, yes, I would. Cause and effect. Either you behave, or something happens." Marion smiled at me indulgently. "I would too!" I protested. "Let's agree on it right now. If a new idea doesn't solve the problem, we throw it out."

"Oh, I agree on that," she said, "but I don't agree to a private children's phone. None of the other parents on this block or any other block would ever forgive us. That's *escalating!* Couldn't we just add an extension on our own phone?"

"That doesn't solve the problem of the constant busy signal."

"Well, I vote we hang up on this debate and go to bed," my wife said.

Of course the kids had too much of an emotional investment in their proposal to give up easily. For a month or more they pursued it day and night, until I was reminded of the way Cato used to conclude all his speeches in the Roman Senate. You recall, no matter what the subject of the speech, he always added the line: "Moreover, I believe that Carthage must be destroyed!" Our kids ended every subject with the plea, "Why can't we have our own telephone?"

Finally my wife said to me, "You know, maybe we ought to let them win this one, just to show that we do play fair."

"Don't be silly," I said, astonished. "They win arguments with us all the time."

"But never on anything important. We always overwhelm them with superior reasoning or experience—or maybe superior force. Now here's an instance where they can see that we really don't like this idea, and yet they have a good case. It *would* solve our phone problems, and if this teaches them anything about living together and sharing, maybe it's worth it on that score, too. Do you suppose we could convince them that their superior logic won, and that they didn't just grind us down by nagging?"

"Are you sure they didn't?"

"No," she said, "but I think we can make this work if we try."

And so we said yes and went out as a family to a grand pizza feast to celebrate. Then we visited the telephone company offices, where Eric and Eve had a marvelous time picking out the color and design of the instruments which would go in each of their rooms, and which would ring simultaneously when a call came in for either of them.

When we got home, we sat them down around the dinner table, and I produced the following document:

Solemn Concordat of Telephone Usage

1. While my parents have agreed to pay the one-time installation charge, I understand that all continuing costs of the phone are to be paid by me, and that henceforth my entire allowance will be withheld for this purpose.
2. I agree to study the Telephone Company's description of toll-free calling areas, and when the phone bill comes in each month to identify all toll calls that I have made, and to pay Dad for them in cash.
3. I agree to use only my own phone for outgoing calls and to give my number to all my friends and *forbid* them, from this time forward, to call me on the family phone.
4. I agree to make it clear to all my friends (and the parents of my friends) that I am paying for this luxury myself, and my parents are not furnishing it.
5. I agree to abide by the Telephone Company's rules and never make joke or nuisance calls, or permit my friends to make them on my phone.
6. I understand that my parents do not intend to answer my phone. If I am home I will answer the phone and courteously take and deliver all messages for my brother or sister.
7. If my brother or sister *is* home I agree to answer the phone if I am physically closer to the instrument, even if we are both downstairs and *I am only one foot nearer the phone;* and I will not argue or grumble about doing so.
8. If my brother or sister wishes to use the phone while I am talking I agree to hang up after five minutes' conversation. Equally, if I wish to use the phone while he or she is using it, I will ask in a quiet and courteous way, and will wait until the five minutes are up.

9. I will never listen in when my brother or sister is talking, or make any comments on the line whatsoever.
10. I understand that any violation of this agreement or any quarreling provoked by the fact of installing this telephone will be cause for instant removal of both phones.

TO ALL OF WHICH I PLEDGE MY WORD, MY BOND,
MY SACRED HONOR.

(signed) _____   (signed) _____
Eve Sanderson   Eric Sanderson

They read it and looked up with silly grins on their faces and asked did they really have to sign it? We said yes, and then gave each a carbon and posted the original on the family bulletin board in the dining room. Two days later their phones were installed.

So, how did it work? Marion and I had our secret doubts, but in fact here we are some years later, and not only is our phone reasonably free and quiet but I can't remember when we've had a fight with the kids about using it. We get to talk to our friends, and our evenings are not ruined jumping up to take messages or to call the kids to the phone. More important, we have given our children a little privacy. We don't need to know, constantly, who's on the other end of the line. Parents interfere too much in the minutiae of their kids' lives because they overhear much of what is said on the family phone.

Eric and Eve have never complained about sacrificing their entire allowance for a telephone. They have made hardly any toll calls, and have paid up promptly when they did; to have teens understand the *economics* of the telephone is a maturing experience in itself. But above all they learned to share a common facility in a civilized way. Yes, they fell into argument a few times, but only twice was I compelled to seize both kids by the arms and march them over to the bulletin board to re-read the Solemn Concordat. Maybe they were due to grow out of the mutual I-hate-you syndrome anyway, but somehow the telephone helped the process along by teaching adult obligations and rights. It surely requires numerous experiences like this to finally produce an Adult at Eighteen, but the lovely part of this small lesson was that we didn't think it up. They did. They had a reason to act in a responsible way.

8 ✽

Is It Possible to Play
With Your Kids?

It's hard work teaching the lessons of life. Most of us sit back advising and admonishing until both we and the kids turn blue with frustration. The trouble is we are essentially *outsiders*. Try as we will at the dinner table, we can't really get far into our kids' daily lives, or bring them into ours. Much of our advice, if it isn't wildly gratuitous, still manages to miss the mark enough to seem partially irrelevant to our children . . . simply because we aren't connected up enough in doing something together that seems important to them.

A century ago when we all lived together on the family farm we could teach in a relatively painless way. But we work in distant places now, doing complex and sophisticated things in which a child can have no part. In our spare time, therefore, any parent with an outside job is simply forced to invent a process of play or recreation which, in a small way, can involve his or her kids to achieve the same ends.

When Eric was thirteen a good friend of mine, Stan Randal, bought a van and then spent several months in our garage outfitting it as living quarters for a safari to Central America. Eric was absolutely fascinated with the planning, design, tools, and material-buying, and the actual construction work. He spent all of his time after school helping Stan, and in fact could hardly chuck down his dinner fast enough to get back to the garage. Ideally I should have joined him, and when it was finished should have found a similar project to enlarge this sudden burst of excitement and learning enthusiasm.

But I never lifted a finger. Why? Converting a van just isn't my thing, I told myself. I don't know anything about it, wouldn't be good at it, and didn't *want* to use my spare time that way. Similarly, when Eric joined the Boy Scouts I thought about becoming actively involved as a Scout leader, but my heart wasn't in it. I went to a few meetings and found that the chief job of the fathers was exacting troop discipline and dragooning reluctant learners into studying for merit badges—the parental function all over again. It was too much like school and home for the boys, and too much like work for me. I suppose if I had been able to take my son and his friends on a true wilderness exploration trip we might have achieved some of the mutual excitement and sharing which could have made it worthwhile, but I had neither the time nor the know-how.

Without really understanding it at the time, however, we had at least one father-son play process going on with marvelous benefits for both of us. It developed by pure accident. The following short article, which appeared in the *New York Times*, explains what happened. (I started out to write a funny piece, but soon realized that every word was literally true.)

The Toughest Football League of Them All

Can a 50-year-old quarterback find happiness trying to out-scramble a 15-year-old linebacker shooting the gap on a hot autumn afternoon when even the tar in the street is melting? Well, he can try. I haven't had a heart attack yet, but let me tell you I went into some kind of a purple funk when I heard that the Raiders were going to retire George Blanda at age 49.

I mean I had the kids on our street convinced that while everybody grows *up*, some of us never grow *old*.

I first got into serious football one Saturday afternoon five years ago when my son burst into the house, his face contorted into the near-apoplexy and tears that only a 10-year-old can manage. "Dad, those guys are *cheating* and ruining the game . . ." Although I was in the middle of some important work for the office—and suddenly recollected that I knew precious little about the rules of today's football—I went out to inspect the pickup touch football game in progress on the street in front of our house.

The trouble, I discovered, was not necessarily cheating but in the fact that my son's team was winning 48–0. Their opponents were either going to score on the next play or they were going home. Every 10-year-old kid is pure Vince Lombardi when it comes to not accepting defeat lightly. I tried to persuade them to choose up sides again and start over, but my son howled that down. I could see his point: after all, the Green Bay Packers in their prime hadn't had to break up *their* winning combination. So I volunteered to help out the weaker team—to actually play and to referee the game, too.

They grumbled some about this but I called an off-side penalty against our team on the first play to prove my bona fides. Then, spotting a weakness in the defense, I faked a pass and handed off to a little beat-up kid in glasses who obviously hadn't touched the ball all afternoon. The defenders were so astounded by this outré choice that my runner scurried around left end untouched.

The radiant astonishment on his face, as he turned in the end zone and spiked the ball, hooked me. I was suddenly in the business of making a few dreams come true, my own included.

The special touch football we have been playing for the past five years developed that day. I immediately ruled out any first-down nonsense—each side had to go all the way from lamp post to lamp post in just four downs. This turned the ball over frequently and kept both teams interested. Secondly, I opened up the game by making every player eligible to do anything, and instituted passball, which allows any player to pass any place on the field, even well beyond the line of scrimmage. Purists may sniff, but let me tell you it's lots of *scoring* which keeps a midget football game alive.

No 10-year-old is interested in doing much blocking on the line, no matter how much you stress team sacrifice, and the quarterbacks on both sides were always getting sacked. The kids themselves devised the rule that a defender had to shout out, "One Mississippi, Two Mississippi, Three Mississippi!" before he could shoot across the line to attack. (One of my tasks as referee was to listen for the mumblers and abbreviators.)

Remembering my own pitiful boyhood in which I never got to carry the ball and nobody ever threw it to me, even though it was *my* football, I put in a rule that every player would take a regular turn at quarterbacking his team for four downs, myself included. In a close game some timid souls were afraid they might fail to produce, but the quarterback fantasy runs early and deep in all males. When I insisted, they did it; and I showed some of the little guys that all they had to do was dump off a short pass to somebody coming out of the backfield, just like Fran Tarkington, and they could go home thinking of themselves as scramblers.

Of course everybody wanted to throw long bombs like Namath, including the occasional father on the street who would come out to join me. "Listen," I told one dad, "they can't catch a pass more than 15 yards out." But he didn't listen. It was a beautiful bomb and it spiraled unerringly between those beseeching outstretched arms of his wide receiver and hit him—*zonko!*—right between the eyes, knocking the boy to the curb. He wasn't really hurt but that *finished* the father. If you can't cope with a few tears—not to mention everybody yelling quarrelsomely at the top of his voice all the time—you just aren't tough enough to play 10-year-old football. Now when *I* throw a bomb it's high and it wobbles and it only goes about 15 yards anyway, so my receivers all think I have a great soft touch.

Of course, as any parent knows, kids don't necessarily respect you just because you're an adult. Not long ago a 13-year-old, who is obviously destined to be a great criminal lawyer, began to dispute some of my calls as referee. "I've got a copy of the rule book," he said, "and you aren't playing right."

"Oh yeah?" I said.

"Yeah."

"Listen," I told him, "if you don't get back on your side of the line and play ball, I'll slap you with a technical."

"A technical!" he howled. "That's basketball."

"Really? Well, you better read paragraph 9A of the Preamble, Subsection 17b, about abusing the umpire." I never thought of the phrase "Delay of Game" until the next day.

For all of us, aspiration exceeded our ability to execute. Freddy, our resident TV student of the game, once called the following play: "I'm going to fake a handoff to you, but I'll spin left. You go out in the flat, while you take out the left end and you decoy deep. Then I pass to Moppy and he laterals back to me, and I fake to whoever hasn't been taken out on the play. Then . . ."

He paused for breath. Everybody in the huddle had gone into shock. "Freddy," I said, "how's that go again?"

He stared at me with frozen dismay. "I forget," he croaked.

Why did I put down my work and walk out in the street that first day? Simply because my son had *asked* me to. It dawned on me that I had turned him down quite a bit lately—I was nearly overwhelmed in organizing a new business at the time. But how often can you stonewall a child before he gives up? Before he gets the message that for one reason or another you simply aren't available to him?

I had no plans to repeat that first football game, but as the whole gang of us sat whooping it up in our kitchen afterwards, drinking Cokes and wolfing down peanut butter and jelly sandwiches as we re-hashed each touchdown, I saw that I had been privileged to enter the private world where my son lived. I'd had a good time almost in spite of myself, and I realized that as an adult I could continue to impose enough order on this neighborhood pickup game to make the competition real, to give my son some feeling of a team participation, the camaraderie of sweat, of working together and sacrificing the ego in a terrible effort toward a shared goal.

We hear so much about Little Leagues, Pop Warner football, YMCA and American Legion teams, and high school sports that we assume that the "team" experience is available to all youth. But it isn't. Probably no more than 5 percent of our sons ever make *any* kind of team, at any time in their lives.

Ours is a complex society in which valuable goals are rarely achieved by single starring efforts. As the years went on, Eric began to see that the object of our football competition was for his team to win, not just for him to personally score more points than the next kid. And so he began to make an increasingly realistic assessment of each team member's skills. It became possible for him to call a play in which he did the blocking and somebody else caught the pass or ran the ball into the end zone.

In part this was possible because he now had an incentive to think about the *nature* of the activity he was involved in. As we watched the professional teams Sunday afternoons on TV the two of us would sometimes spot a play which might be adapted to our street game. We'd get pencil and paper to diagram it, and sometimes we'd rehearse it in the living room.

Here father and son were functioning as equals. I wasn't the parent telling him how it had to be; we were discovering and learning together. With the lines of communication wide open between us in this neutral ground, it was possible for the conversation casually to shift to other areas of his life. I discovered things about school, for example, that I never would have heard otherwise, because a kid's defenses go up automatically under the normal parental quizzing. And—would you believe—in later years we actually talked about girls and sex occasionally? No big deal—just a casual question and answer here and there during the commercials, when our conversation happened to shift that way.

I think, too, that the football game gave him his first true opportunity to test himself as a group leader. Eric was not necessarily the best athlete, but because of our joint analysis of the plays he was more *aware* of what was going on. He learned to intervene in the decision-making process to suggest new and more promising lines of play, and gradually the team began to listen to him.

So many kids have trouble accepting authority these days. But it occurs to me that young men who have had a prolonged experience playing on a team of some kind have less trouble. They come to see that some rules are essential, and the beauty and the satisfaction of the game structure are marred unless the rules are enforced. When a young person comes to understand that absolute liberty leads to absolute chaos he is halfway down the road to maturity.

I was fascinated to see Eric's growing impatience with the whiners, the alibi-artists, the goof-arounds, the grudge-carriers, and the angry little boys perpetually crying foul. He wanted the team to function and to win, and he began to see that the ego trips and the personal hangups of some members destroyed the cohesiveness necessary for group success.

In the beginning it just about ruined Eric's day if his team lost, but after several years of campaigning I began to make a dent in the "winning is everything" attitude. Nice guys who try harder usually win *next* time—especially if they've made the effort to invent some new plays to surprise the opposition. But in any case every young person has to understand that each action in our lives should be invested with an appropriate emotion. This was only a private game among friends, not the Super Bowl. The sooner this fine scale of proportion is learned the happier any child—or adult—becomes.

And this includes the art of winning gracefully. It was almost harder to cut down the gloating, the boastfulness, and the put-downs. But gradually the winners stopped preening and strutting quite so much and we even began to develop a style of applauding a super play during the game, even though we'd been badly faked-out or simply outrun.

As he gained a sense of proportion, Eric increasingly began to accept the idea that the little kids and the gawky dum-dums with glasses who stumbled over their own feet and were forever offside also had a right to play with us, even if they did diminish the quality of the game. My son never got over wanting desperately to win, but sometimes he would take a chance and throw a hopeful ball to a player we all knew would drop it, and sometimes I would see him pull into the huddle some little kid who had obviously been left out of the action for a long time.

Will these insights about winning & losing and the ways in which people function in a group help him to understand the adult world? I don't know—I hope so. Meanwhile I had quite a lot of fun myself.

9 ✳

The Importance of Being
Not-So-Earnest

One summer when Lisa was away working and Eric and Eve were at camp, Marion and I suddenly found ourselves living a purely adult life. What a vacation! We had all our time and all our emotions to ourselves; our days suddenly seemed so ordered, so peaceful, so pleasantly selfish. But after several weeks we slowly became aware that things weren't the same as in the early days of marriage. We *weren't* just two people any more; we were a family. And two parts of the family operating alone didn't seem to be enough. We began to violate our pact not to talk about the kids, and one evening when we couldn't stand it any longer, we even decided to sit down and write them a joint letter, recounting the family and neighborhood news, and also saying how much we liked and admired each of them. Parents don't do this as often as they think about doing it, we decided.

In addition to specific affirmations of love, it seems to me that parents should also attempt to communicate to their kids the nature of the generational relationship. Many teenagers, listening to the troubles their friends have with their parents, assume that their own parents are also grossly unable to understand what it's all about. Sometimes this is purely an *intellectual* rationalization; underneath, on the emotional level, they may actually feel they have quite a sympathetic relationship with their parents.

It never hurts to remind our kids that although we may be twenty-five or thirty years older, we can still remember what it was like to be young, and that we're pretty good at adapting from what was Then to what is Now. That, in fact, lots of things don't change that much.

Here is a portion of what I wrote in the letter to all three kids that day:

Twinkie, Twinkie, Little Cake . . .
I Love You Tho You Are a Fake

DEAR KIDS:

At a dinner party the other night your mother and I and several other couples began to speculate about generation gaps—specifically whether there was a greater distance today between parent and child than in the previous generations. We agreed that while you may occasionally think we are as obtuse and irrelevant as triceratops (and twice as mean), in fact we have a better understanding by far of *your* world than your grandparents ever did of *ours*.

We developed a lot of thoughtful reasons why this is so. For example, mobility. We were the first generation to casually jump in an old car and drive across the country, just to see what was out there. And it wasn't anybody in our generation who said: If God had meant man to fly he would have put wings on his heels. We knew instinctively that we were meant to ride the heavens as if we owned them, and could never fall.

We were the first of the media generations: Radio and movies taken together probably had as big an effect on our fantasy lives as TV has had on yours. The great population shift from farm to urban areas also occurred during our generation, with its infinite ramifications; and the nation managed enough prosperity so that a "teen culture" developed for the first time in human history. Ours wasn't as full-blown as yours—I only had a portable windup phonograph, for example, but we all listened to the Hit Parade on Saturday night radio so we'd know what to buy down at the Record Rack Monday after school.

It wasn't until I picked up the *Wall Street Journal* this morning, however, that I realized the real, true bond between your time and mine. *We were the first generation to get hooked on junk food.*

Yea, verily. Now I have no idea what my father ate when he was a kid—probably whatever was put before him. But let me tell you that when I was in high school and occasionally required to prepare my own supper—are you ready for this?—my meal, without exception, consisted of: one entire can of Franco-American spaghetti and one bag of potato chips, *and one package of Twinkies.* Now any parent with a background of vice like that can't be all bad, right?

Oh yes, I washed it all down with a quart of milk—because nobody was rich enough to buy soft drinks for the refrigerator in those days. The Pepsi generation actually began in our time. Can you believe one of the first singing commercials on radio still runs through my mind?

> Pepsi-Cola hits the spot,
> Twelve full ounces—that's a lot.
> Twice as much for a nickel too,
> Pepsi-Cola is the drink for you!

Nickel . . . nickel . . . nickel . . . nickel . . . nickel . . .

I think there were five "nickels" at the fadeout. "Twice as much" refers to the fact that Coca-Cola had always been sold in the familiar 6¾ oz. bottle, whereas upstart Pepsi offered 12 oz. for the same price, an important consideration. They both tasted the same then as they do now. Nor has Franco-American spaghetti become a food that might be recognized in either

France or Italy. Or Campbell's Cream of Mushroom Soup, which I then sometimes had for breakfast. Years later when I finally got to France it took me months to learn to like *real* mushroom soup.

But that wasn't what the *Wall Street Journal* article was about. Oh, no. There it was on Page 1, a whole article devoted to Twinkies! How significant can a food get as a national symbol? The secret passion of my childhood has now become America's largest selling "cake"—700,000,000 Twinkies a year! Even Archie Bunker eats them. Archie's pout when Edith forgets to put a Twinkie in his lunchpail always draws a big laugh, according to the *Journal*. Just in case anybody is so oblivious (or so *old*) that he doesn't know what a Twinkie is, the *Journal* defines it as a "small sponge cake, roughly half the size of a fat knockwurst, filled with a sugary, creamy confection." The Wonder Bread people have been making Twinkies since 1930, but have never claimed that Twinkies will build up your body in eleven ways, which is lucky because the most important ingredient in Twinkies is sugar. Even so, one man in Los Angeles reportedly lived on Twinkies and Cutty Sark exclusively for seven years. He finally died when hit by a car, and the *Journal* implied that it might have been because he was under the influence of a Twinkie.

Students in Rochester, Minnesota, staged a three-day First Annual International Twinkie Festival, which included events such as Twinkie-eating, naming, and petting, Twinkie sculpture, a Twinkie recipe contest and treasure hunt, and a derby in which Twinkies were fixed up with toothpick axles and wheels, and raced. A Twinkie was even attached to 300 balloons filled with helium and sent up to outer space— heavenly food where it belongs, they said.

The college itself sponsored the festival but said a second International Twinkie Festival wouldn't be held because it "would only detract from the significance of the first." Somehow I like the spirit of that school.

Anyway, the point of all this was the question of the generation gap. The answer seems obvious to me because, after all, what did *my* old man ever know about Twinkies?

Well, all right, that was fun, and the kids seemed to like it. Why am I telling you all this? I don't know, except that a lot of kids have difficulty imagining *their* old man standing around in the kitchen munching on a Twinkie, much less appreciating the fantasy of "petting" one or racing it. Too many fathers make a point of never being caught out of their dignity, of allowing themselves to suspend judgment for a few moments as to what is real and useful. It *is* hard for one generation to participate in another's humor; perhaps it is enough if we show that at least we have listened well enough to recognize their sense of the absurd, and that we are not so calcified that we have to dismiss it with disdain.

A little frivolity, a few jokes, a bit of horseplay can never hurt, even if it is out of date as far as our kids are concerned. Every time we display our humanity we increase, rather than diminish, our authority as parents. We can't teach unless they are willing to listen, and many elements of what we have to say can only be communicated by indirection. The message flows out of us unconsciously and is received in the same manner when both parents and kids are in good spirits.

Many fathers feel they have a good "kidding" relationship with their children, but unless great conscious care is shown "kidding" can easily become "needling." For example, I have a friend who is a free-lance commercial artist; on the wall above his drawing table at home are pinned a number of sketches from his current work. Recently I saw a small hand-lettered sign among them:

NEVER TRUST ANYONE OVER THIRTY. HE MAY
ADVISE YOU TO DO SOMETHING DIFFICULT.

—Sophocles

This little sign has a certain humorous impact from one parent to another, but of course it was intended for my friend's teenage kids. I doubt if they think it's funny. It suggests a nagging disappointment, and it raises a barrier. Our kids are not equipped to contest with us in many arenas; they can't invent Sophoclean epigrams, for example. But they do know how to turn off, how to resist silently. Many fathers in the competitive outside world develop a needling game with other adult males. This is simply an exercise in cut-and-parry, masked with humor. It may do no harm and serve to keep equal adult opponents in fighting trim, but it is destructive when carried over into the parent-child relationship.

They are so defenseless that I believe every father ought to make a rule never to kid with his children about a serious subject. It is too easily perceived as an attack. All joking or joshing should be *with*, not *at* them; and it should be pretty well confined to neutral areas in which neither side has a strong emotional investment. Many parents, especially fathers, feel so frustrated and helpless before the passive resistance of their kids that they use the sardonic gibe as one of the few ways to get through the kids' skin. If it provokes a response, well, at least that's *something*. But it isn't; a forced retort in kind may simply make the child feel more angry and inadequate.

Our children can never open up to us except in the brief spells when we lift the confrontation, when we express unequivocal love and approval, and block out any subconscious disappointment that our kids are not the perfect fulfillment of our dreams.

10 ✳

Fighting "Sexism" at Home— It's Not So Easy

My wife and I and the three children were sitting at the dinner table one night when Eve (age thirteen) suddenly said, "I think I want to be a dental hygienist."

"Oh?" we chorused.

"Why settle for that?" Lisa demanded. "The dentist filled your cavity and checked the work of the hygienist after she was finished. *He's* the boss. Why don't you want to be him?"

"I couldn't do that," Eve answered uncertainly.

"Why not? He had to go to college and then to dental school, like a doctor. But women can do that. Women don't have to be just assistants to men."

We understood, of course. The hygienist she had seen that day was a young and pretty girl, barely twenty-one, with a loving smile and childlike simplicity; and she had fussed over Eve. The dentist had been friendly enough, but busy and professional. He was, above all, a male, balding, old enough to be her father. She could not see herself in his image.

We were delighted to find Lisa so charged with the sense of her own unlimited potential. Sheer weariness, I suppose, dismayed us that we still had so far to go with Eve. Parents are always forgetting that every child is a new world, and what you have done for one does not necessarily carry over to another. But of course Eve was only barely into her teens; why should we have expected any other attitude?

Every thoughtful parent today is concerned about breaking sexual stereotypes. Women's liberation is not a joke, it is simple justice. Our sons had better understand the meaning of the word "sexist," because the women they marry and the women they meet in their career world will be far different people from their mothers. For this reason parents should confront the issue openly and constantly, encouraging the children themselves to question sex-role assumptions, to keep asking: "Do I have to think about this matter differently just because I'm a girl or boy?"

Many foreign languages arbitrarily assign a gender to each noun, pronoun, and adjective. Part of our role as parents in today's world is to encourage our children to drop this kind of useless baggage. Most things, most actions, must functions, most feelings do not have gender in actuality, and we are only complicating and narrowing life by accepting these unreal limitations.

Once again, our children learn from us. As teens, they have already absorbed many of our unconscious attitudes toward the opposite sex; these attitudes have already been built into their sexual identities. But there is still work we can do, since we ourselves are changing in response to the demands of our society. Both mother and father have accumulated most sexist attitudes than they know, and it is only by dragging them out into the open in specific, even trivial situations that we get to examine them clearly. The mere effort to try to teach our children sexual justice may in fact make us more just.

For example, in conveying to the kids that no sex role is attached to such household chores as mowing the lawn and washing dishes, I had to demonstrate that it was not inappropriate for me to make a bed, vacuum a rug, shop at the supermarket, or take out the garbage, even if (because of the pressures of my workweek) I didn't do it all the time, or even very often. Every husband and wife develop a division of labor in their marriage, and this agreement should be verbalized for the children to see. If one spouse works long hours Monday through Friday as the sole bread-earner, it will seem fair to them that he or she deserves some relief from household duties. If both spouses work, it will seem fair that male and female divide the domestic chores equally. But in any case work is work and a chore is a chore, and no sexual identification is involved.

It's hard to realize how many sex-role questions we face each day. For example, every house has a lawn, and mowing is *male* work. But why? Probably because a few generations ago mowing meant the harvesting of crops, and it was heavy, sweaty labor. (Similarly, father drives the family car because that's his "role." Two generations ago it made sense because a team of horses required some physical strength to handle—they could run away on you.) Anyway, I was too busy myself to mow lawns and wasn't about to hire a neighbor boy when I had a perfectly fit teenage body available. So in the early years Lisa did the mowing. Although she seldom got out the mower except under duress, it was not because she thought it was a boy's job; like most teens, she simply didn't want to do *any* work around the house.

A few years later we had in mind that Eve should replace Lisa with the yardwork, and Eric should help with the dishes. But nothing in family life works out this neatly. When the time came, Eric was strong enough to push the mower and Eve wasn't. So she became her mother's inside assistant. We tried to attack this stereotype and once, a year later, Eric and Eve actually agreed to switch work assignments. But it was too late: they were both furious and demanded their old jobs back.

Eric finally did take over the dishes for a few months, however. As I mentioned, he was hard up for spending money until he got his paper route, and since Eve was coining surplus cash as a baby-sitter, she paid him to do her dishes. He charged a tough price, but she didn't quibble. We thought this a useful lesson for both. She learned that you can hire people to do domestic work if you've got a better-paying job. He learned that when you're needy you have to take whatever work is available—and, anyway, dishes don't have gender.

I tried to persuade Eric that baby-sitting might solve his money problem, but none of his friends had ever done this kind of work. Nevertheless, one night when Eve was already busy I told a frantic mother on the telephone that Eric would help her out. No babies were involved, just two small boys. Eric left in black anger but came home in a rather serene mood, clutching his cash—the easiest money he'd ever earned. After that he gladly accepted Eve's overflow sitter jobs and even developed a few clients of his own.

The football game in the street also provided an opening for "consciousness-raising." One day Eric and his gang and I were in the middle of a noisy fourth down when Eve and three of her girl friends, about nine or ten years old, gathered on the curb and began to imitate the high school cheerleaders. We males were flattered, of course, but I thought how sad it was that the female supporting role should begin at this age. Weren't they ever going to be the *players* in the game?

"Come on," I said, "it's only touch football and you girls can run as fast as the boys."

"*What!*" the boys howled. "Play with girls? No way!" The cheerleaders were intimidated and backed away.

But I outyelled everybody. "Listen!" I cried, "I'll be on the girls' side and I bet we can beat you!" That did it. Of course we didn't actually win the first time, but we scored a few touchdowns and kept the game close, and all of us felt satisfied. From then on I was even able to persuade the boys to accept mixed boy-girl teams, and we played together for two seasons.

At first the boys expected to run everything, but I enforced the rule that *everybody* on a team had to take a turn at quarterback, want to or not. A girl didn't have to run the ball or throw it necessarily, but she had to think up the play and give everybody his assignment. Did this work? You have to see a timid little creature blossom when a group of males solemnly listens to her in the huddle and then goes out and obeys without question.

Eve and I had a pretty good combination going. Her favorite play was the B.C. Special. Originally designed for Johnny Unitas of the Baltimore Colts, it went like this: Eve as quarterback would take the ball from center, fake a handoff to the left, but actually slip it to me. I'd run for a right-end sweep, pulling the defenders toward me, but just as I was about to be tagged I'd turn and toss the ball back to Eve, who had remained in her original position. She was now wide open to throw a fine left-handed spiral to our favorite receiver, Betty-Marie, who wasn't very fast but could always manage to gather the ball to her motherly bosom as she chugged across the goal line.

We had just scored on this play one perfect Saturday afternoon, and were jumping and hollering and hugging each other, when reality closed in. We looked up to see two of Eve's friends, perhaps a year or so older, watching from the sidewalk. They wore frilly party dresses, with their hair artfully tied, and I think they even had on a touch of eye shadow. They looked very feminine. One of them smiled, and then, with just the faintest shrug of disdain, they strolled away. Our sweaty girls in their T-shirts and ragged shorts stared at each other; and it was never the same again. The girls played a few more times, but their hearts weren't with us; they kept looking over their shoulders. And the boys couldn't understand what was happening.

Thus begins a pattern which, it seems to me, recurs again and again in a girl's development. Certainly I've seen it often enough in the business world. The males, after they get over the initial shock of finding a female where none had been before, more often than not accept a woman at face value. If she can do the job, if she is what she says she is, if she demands no special privileges, then women's liberation simply becomes a fact of life. It's the female who sometimes spoils the new freedom, either because she doesn't have a strong enough belief in her own powers or because another female tells her—one way or another—that she is not acting with appropriate femininity.

The problem, obviously, is to build enough strength and understanding into a daughter so that she doesn't falter under pressure, doesn't sell herself short, doesn't retreat under the reproaches of weaker females. Adult at Eighteen should help to do this—it is the most determinedly non-sexist position that parents can take. We never allow a girl to grow up weak and dependent. We require her to take charge of herself in an appropriate way, to be adult, to be responsible, and there is no way we can treat a girl differently from a boy in this sense.

Couldn't Marion and I convince Eve that it was OK to enjoy a hot, sweaty team sport sometimes? That doing this wouldn't preclude her being a dainty, attractive female at other times? The pressures of a hundred generations are against us, and they are all reflected in teen peer-group approval. If we want a young girl to be free we not only have to fight against our own unrecognized prejudices but against the sex-role stereotypes projected by all the other parents and children. So, let's face it, you can only go so far.

We decided we would do what we could short of pushing Eve into situations which would bring ridicule by her age group. Since Lisa was a freshman in college at this point, much respected by Eve, we asked Lisa if she wouldn't join us in some "girl liberation." In our rapidly changing world five or six years is half a generation; Lisa could speak with authority on every aspect of manners and mores which might bother a young girl.

Above all, we wanted Eve to gain a more positive image of herself as to what kind of work she might do in the world—thirteen is *not at all* too early. Lisa sent away for an excellent book * which briefly describes 150 or so jobs and careers, tells how women can get into them, what education is needed, what the salaries and chances for promotion are, and where to find more detailed information in each field. Together they sat down to go through it. I can hear Lisa now, reading aloud the section on "Welder (Joins metal parts to-

---

* *I Can Be Anything: Careers and Colleges for Young Women*, by Joyce Slayton Mitchell (College Board Publication Orders, Box 2815, Princeton, N.J. 08540).

gether by applying heat, pressure, or both, with or without filler metal to produce a permanent bond)."

What's It Like to Be a Welder?

"All the skills my school told me would make me a perfect typist—finger dexterity, eye-hand coordination, form and space perception—are exactly the same skills that make me a well-paid and happy welder," writes Judy King. "I love working in a shop and never would have stayed in an office job. When I was in high school I started in the secretarial course and tried to convince the vocational teacher that I wanted to learn welding. After finally convincing him and learning the skill I had no trouble getting a job because I demonstrated to the boss how well I could do the work." Since that time, a high school girl has won the national welding competition for trade school students. Ms. King says there is no comparison in the money she makes and the money made by her friends who have office jobs and the same level of education. She wishes more high school girls knew about welding so they could get in on it too.

"But I don't want to be a welder," Eve protested.

"That's all right," Lisa answered. "I just want you to understand that it's OK to be a welder—it's not just a man's job. Look, here it tells about a woman in Cleveland who is not only an electrician herself but hires other women who have families to work part time in doing home repairs. Remember the other day dad had to call in an electrician when all the fuses blew? That could have been a woman."

"It could have?"

"Sure, why not? The electrician had to learn his trade somehow and a woman can be just as bright and just as good with her hands. An electrician doesn't have to lift two-hundred-pound weights or anything like that."

"I don't think I want to be an electrician," Eve said.

"I don't either, as it happens. But everybody ought to have a right to do their own thing and not be ashamed of it, don't you think? These are good jobs that make good money, and women ought to have an equal chance at them, right? Look, you're pretty good in science. Do you know what a physicist does?"

And then I heard them working through Foreign Service officer, city planner, actuary, astronomer, forester, and business executive, among others.

A few sessions with an older sister, of course, is not enough to break a stereotype. Like anything else in parental education, it's a drip-drip-drip process. Ten thousand separate inputs of information, ten thousand times an attitude is expressed. Marion and I were forever clipping out articles from newspapers and magazines which showed how a woman started up a business of her own or was promoted to become chief troubleshooter in a computer industry or won a Nobel Prize for genetic research.

When she was a senior in high school, Lisa still had not expressed any clear idea of what she wanted as a career, except that it wasn't going to be in science, medicine, or the arts. So I told her she really ought to be thinking about what kind of jobs in business she might like, because that's where most of the jobs *are;* and if she didn't start thinking about it (just as a male does), she might end up as somebody's secretary.

Women often see this as a sexist conspiracy, but in fact until the current generation it was a rare woman who aspired to a business career or believed, in her soul, that she *could* assume power and leadership in what had always been a male world. Whether we approve or not, the business of America has often been business. It's the mainstream of our national life, and unless a woman psychologically conditions herself to believe she can function there at a high level she's going to be shut out. Equal opportunity only means opportunity for people with equal desire.

But how do you *get* desire? Entirely aside from what the parents can inject, it is obviously important to have specific role models. Lisa, with great clarity, had pointed out that she wasn't much interested in a business career because she didn't know many women who were making a great success in it. Even if she could "make it," she wondered, wouldn't she have to sacrifice a good deal of her femininity and other human values in the process?

Since this is certainly a normal apprehension, the only answer was for Lisa to meet some women in business and ask them how they felt about it. I called up a few male friends. Did they know any rising female executives in their own companies whom they also admired as people? And would these women have time to talk to a dubious high school girl?

I wasn't too hopeful about this project at first. Frankly, Lisa and I hadn't had much chance to get together by ourselves for a while, so I thought this would be a good excuse to have lunch in town with my daughter. But my friends were surprisingly enthusiastic (maybe because they were fathers themselves). It turned out that everyone had one or two young women in his company who he thought were *terrific*. Sure, they'd be glad to see her. Just name the date.

And so Lisa and I walked into the offices of a lot of strange women and asked them to explain how they had got where they were in advertising, marketing, manufacturing, sales, personnel, and research. I tagged along on the first few interviews because Lisa was somewhat nervous, and I was also afraid the women might be a bit stiff with her; it was, after all, a kind of command performance from the boss in several cases.

As it turned out, these businesswomen were tremendously supportive of the idea that girls need to understand what kind of jobs are possible today. I think Lisa immediately felt the "sisterhood" they expressed as they explained what schools they'd gone to and how they got their first job, and what it took to get promoted. They were also surprisingly candid about the pressures of the job, and how it affected their personal lives. But in every one of them we found pride and exuberance in what she was doing. They liked their work and they were going to succeed at it. Lisa and I came away charged up not only about the individuals but about the system itself, which was beginning to open to let a woman reach as high as she could.

I'm sure any parent can arrange his own interviews in a more natural way than I did, covering a period of years as the teen daughter grows up. When we stop to look, there are successful career women all around us, and it is extremely important to find living proof that a girl can have a good job and aspire to the top without abandoning the other great natural joys of being a woman.

11 ✳

Telling Them How It Was With Us

Since our children have to deal with us as Authority, any evidence they can unearth as to what we're *really* like helps them to respond to our power—or to evade it. As role models we fascinate them, partly out of desire to be exactly like us, partly out of a passionate determination *not* to resemble us at all.

This is a valuable struggle, and we can make it easier for them by offering more information. It's one thing to tell them how we are thinking-feeling-acting now as mature adults, but we get quite a different response when we lift the velvet curtain of the past and try to remember aloud just how it was with us when we were their ages. Recently TV and films have helped to set the stage for us as they feature stories about young people growing up in the 1940s and 1950s. Our time was different, all right, but it no longer seems quite so exotic to a teenager today; he knows some of the ways we dressed and talked then, and if we give him an honest scenario (with a little plot) he may even be able to identify with us.

And that's what we want them to do, isn't it? To think: my parents were actually dumb scared kids just like me, and they had their problems too, and they managed to get through them. When they went out into the world they didn't know what to expect, but they weren't afraid to speak up and ask for what they wanted. They kept struggling, and eventually they won. They were *accepted*.

It is hard to know which of our experiences will appeal to our children. Apparently it just can't be a conscious process—you open up, and they let you know if you have scored any points. Once I got talking about my first frightened days in the Marine Corps during World War II; I think I had in the back of my mind that I wanted to encourage Lisa to assert herself—to show that once in a while an almost foolhardy blurting out of the truth is justified. And also that the sheer shock value of outrageous presumption can sometimes carry you through a difficult situation. Anyway, to my surprise, the following two anecdotes turned out to be favorites with the entire family.

Too Scared to Fail

I must have been one of the shakiest officer candidates the Marine Corps ever had. To begin with I was only eighteen years old, and rather scrawny, pimply, and pale. I had astonished myself by enlisting in the Marines, and somehow on the strength of some good test scores and one precocious year in college they had assigned me to OCS. Like all the services in the middle of the war, the Marines were expanding furiously and probably some bureaucrat in Washington didn't know what he was getting when he picked me. Anyway, there was a current saying in the Corps that when it came to storming the beaches of the South Pacific good sergeants went in the *second* wave, because they were hard to come by. Callow young second lieutenants were first down the ramp, since they were in such generous supply.

Why had I joined the Marines? Because they were *men*, I guess. I must have felt that I had to prove something to a lot of people because I dimly remember feeling that if I couldn't go home a certified Leader of Men, a second lieutenant of Marines, the roughest of the tough, I wasn't going home at all. Maybe *ever*. How foolish can you get? See how much brighter you kids are than we were in those days?

Unfortunately, somewhere in the second week of OCS training I began to realize I was not doing well at all. I had accumulated a horrendous number of demerits, and already members of our class were disappearing, shipped out in the night as privates, replacements in rifle companies that were being shot up on Pacific beaches. "Only about half of you people are strong enough and mean enough and smart enough to make it to graduation," the cadre had warned us, and as I looked around at the men remaining I got the dismal impression that they were not listing me among the survivors.

We were sitting at tables in an abandoned mess hall listening to a lecture on the theory of the U.S. Browning .30 light machine gun, and I was getting panicked. We not only had to pass written tests on this and other weapons, but also had to be able to take them apart and put them together blindfolded. The instructor was pouring out stuff like: "*The extractor cam plunger which rides along the top of the extractor cam and the extractor feed cam is finally forced in by the beveled section of the extractor feed cam. The cover extractor cam thus forces the extractor down and the plunger springs out behind the extractor feed cam which . . .*"

He went on like this for a half hour and, although I had spent half the night with the manual, my mind froze. This is *insane*, I thought. Who can follow this double-speak? Unaccountably, there wasn't a disassembled machine gun in sight so that we could follow the lecture. For some minutes I studied the other candidates around me. They didn't seem to be nervous about this incomprehensible recital; they were all paying strict attention.

Without quite realizing what I was doing, I got slowly to my feet. The lecturer stopped in mid-sentence, astonished. "Yes?" he said.

"Excuse me, sir," I croaked, "but I don't know what the hell you're talking about." Out of the corner of my eyes I saw the cadre officers scattered about the edge of the room pick up their pencils and those dreaded individual report pads; several craned to read the name which was stenciled in three-inch letters front and back across our fatigue uniforms. So then I knew it was over: this runty, beat-up kid had blown it. He had confessed weakness to this group of super-toughs. "We need the guns to look at while he's talking!" I cried desperately. "Nobody can learn this way!"

I was speaking for myself, of course, but, do you know, a marvelous thing happened. In what seemed a single exhalation the entire battalion breathed out a fervent, approving "*Yeaah!*"

"What? You mean you college geniuses can't—"

"YEAAAH!" they chorused again, even louder, and full of solidarity. "*Give us the guns!*" So great was my relief and gratitude that tears welled up, a fact that I desperately hoped nobody noticed . . . And in the end we got a disassembled weapon for each table, and I assumed (we never knew for sure) that I had scored a few *good* chits for leadership and sheer bravado. Oliver Twist had dared to ask for more.

It was a lesson I remembered all my life, kids. You, too, will find yourself in the middle of any number of patently absurd conditions in the next few years—both in college and later. Don't tolerate situations which violate all our views of reality, justice, or just plain common sense. If you are being asked to praise the emperor and he really doesn't have any pants on, take a chance. *Speak up.* It's almost certain that other people have noticed too, and they will be terribly relieved (maybe even grateful) that somebody dared assert himself.

Tell some more about the Marines? Well, let's see. I survived the weapons training, but then I began to have trouble with what they called "Command Presence." Whatever that was, I didn't have it. Not only did I not look like a Leader of Men, I didn't feel like one. Some of the veterans in our battalion had been selected for officer training straight out of jungle combat with the Japanese—*they* knew what it was all about. Then there were the college football jocks, wrestlers and weight-lifters literally twice my size, plus an assortment of older man-of-the-world Ivy League fraternity types.

Not only did I not possess a samurai sword which I had personally wrested out of an enemy hand, I also didn't know "pass" from "fade" in craps or how to negotiate with a girl of very little virtue (I had never met one). I got sick when I drank beer, and I was the only man in our barracks who didn't sleep in his government-issued underwear—I wore civilian pajamas. And I read books in my spare time. Even worse, I had a rather immature, girlish voice which provoked guffaws when I took my turn at leading close-order drill.

To remedy this I began to creep out into the woods after taps to rehearse a steady baritone. For a quarter of an hour or so I would bellow out "Right flank, march!" and "Column left!" and "Company dismissed!" from as deep in the belly as I could muster. At last, just as I was beginning to enjoy the sound of my own voice, I spotted two jeeploads of MPs, spotlights blazing, hurtling down the trail toward me. In order to avoid being heard by my fellow candidates I had apparently penetrated so deeply into the woods that I had approached, unknowingly, a female Marine barracks on the other side. "Some lunatic has been out there for three nights running, baying at the moon," they had reported. Or else it was a demented troop howling in sexual frustration.

After some helter-skelter hide & seek in the woods I escaped and, nothing daunted, the next day volunteered once again as drillmaster before I lost my new voice. With all the giddy desperation of a man who had been running too long on thin ice, I decided that if I had failed as a platoon and company commander I had to make up for everything by drilling the whole damn battalion!

All went well at first. I had got the rhythm and cadence down right and the men seemed to accept me. I was conservative in my maneuvers, and the commands themselves sounded sonorous enough to me. "OK, turn 'em around and bring them back to the barracks," the captain said finally. Sweet words to a troubled soul; I had apparently triumphed. But to cause 280 men to reverse direction on a single beat is no easy task; and without my noticing it a brisk wind had blown up. The first two companies heard my "To the rear!" command perfectly and wheeled sharply to march pell-mell into the face of the rest of the battalion which either hadn't heard the word, or pretended not to.

Absolute chaos! Grinning, jostling, cursing: it was a military mob scene as half the battalion tried to march south and the rest in other directions . . . Now they were all enjoying my disaster, and every officer on the sidelines was writing a negative chit.

To this moment I don't understand what happened next, except that sheer hysteria took over. I began to shriek at them: "Why, you mangy, splay-eyed, lop-eared, stub-tailed sons of she-goats, you wouldn't know your left from your right if you had six toes on one foot and took off your shoes to count! You miserable . . ." I was suddenly the British drillmaster dressing down his Indian recruits in *Gunga Din* and *The Charge of the Light Brigade*. Then I was John Wayne, with improvisations, beating back his bolting troops in *Bataan*. "Form up! Stop milling around! Act like *men*—we haven't begun to fight!" All the dialogue and invective, relevant or not, which I had stored up during a lonely, dreamy youth spent in darkened movie houses spewed forth. I ranted, raved, and cursed, standing hands on hips like a little Napoleon, bouncing on the balls of my feet, absolutely and literally out of my mind. I had never done anything like this before—nor have I since.

Slowly I became aware that I had stilled them; I had their attention. And then, to my surprise, I saw some of the officers smiling. I had unwittingly blundered into an old Marine tradition, chewing ass, in which the drill instructor or officer vents his spleen at the passive-aggression of troops determined to get things wrong. Tradition allowed the raging officer to blow his top for just so long as he could come up with original things to say, and nobody had *ever* before heard my movie version . . . At last I had the battalion fall out and stand into a new formation, dress up, and after that we marched back to the barracks in perfect order. Even then I feared to halt my harangue.

When I had dismissed the battalion, my eye met our major as he stood conferring with his officers, his hands full of my chits and a puzzled but respectful half-frown on his face. His attitude seemed to be saying that I must be some kind of wild-yelling eighteen-year-old purple moon animal . . . but he wasn't absolutely sure the Marine Corps shouldn't have at least one in its ranks.

What this story proves, dear kids, I don't quite know. Maybe it's that you should never accept defeat without Asserting Yourself, no matter how badly things seem to be going. Or maybe the moral is that we can all be just as crazy as we have to be to break out of encircling disaster.

12 ✳

Memo to a Daughter: Some Thoughts About Indulging Yourself

DEAR EVE:

I wonder if you even remember now that we stopped bugging you about your eating habits three years ago? Acting on the Premise of Eighteen, we decided that eating really was your responsibility, not ours. Frankly, this was not an enormously statesmanlike decision on our part; short of locking you in your room and force-feeding you with a tube there simply was no way we could compel you to ingest the delightful and nutritionally balanced meals your mother fixed. If it didn't have pizza in it you weren't interested, so we opted for a little tranquillity at the dinner table.

Oh, if we'd thought your teeth were going to fall out for lack of some mineral or vitamin, I suppose we'd have taken action. But somehow your body probably got most of the elements it needed. In fact, in view of your recent comment to your mother, you seem to think your body is taking in *more* than you need. Dear daughter, you don't look fat to me, but based on your absolutely lousy eating habits I don't see how you can avoid putting on weight sooner or later.

Did you ever see the diet suggestions I wrote out for Lisa when she was a senior in high school? Like you, she wasn't fat, but she had your eating pattern and sure enough it finally began to show. When her clothes didn't fit very well and she didn't like the way she looked, she finally began to think about calories. We will still love you if you get fat, and your friends may not object terribly, even your boy friends. It's your self-image that counts. If you can't stand the idea of "pudgy," then *don't get fat*. It's so easy not to put on weight at your age, and so *hard* to take it off later. Insurance companies say that more than eighty million Americans are at least ten pounds overweight because we indulge ourselves constantly. Look around you—look at the beginning fatties in the young people you know. Don't be a statistic.

Here is what I wrote for Lisa. It's not really a diet regime— just some common sense about what you put in your mouth.

A general theory holds among American parents that if kids would stop eating "all that junk" between meals they would never suffer from poor nutrition or overweight. Parental instincts are right, as usual; but also as usual this doesn't necessarily solve your problem. The unhappy fact is you adore junk food (so do I, I'm sorry to say). You like it so well that you probably take in more calories in snacking, both in and out of the home, than you do in regular meals.*

So what does this mean—do you have to give it all up to avoid gaining weight? No. But you have to give up *some* of it, some of the time. Surprisingly little, really, but even this much may seem painful to you at first. Right here comes one of the really important lessons in adulthood: *you can't have everything.* Nobody can ever have everything she wants, because human wants are inexhaustible.

---

* For example, did you know that at one leading hamburger chain the large burger adds 550 calories to your daily intake? And a chocolate shake runs 520 calories, a small order of french fries at least 200, and a soft drink 100–200? The average full meal you eat at home will contain only *two-thirds* as many calories—maybe fewer— including dessert.

Trouble is, up to now in your life you actually have had almost everything you ever wanted. Middle-class kids have been denied almost *nothing* (certainly not food) for up to fifteen or twenty years of their lives.

Suddenly, here is something your parents can't give you. They can't give you slimness. You have to make it yourself. And so you discover one of the most important rules of life: *short-term gratifications often have to be sacrificed for larger long-term goals.*

Every time you can identify a worthy goal and make the effort and sacrifice necessary to achieve it you become a stronger person. So, be a successful dieter—among other things. Here are some ways to begin thinking about it:

The Practically Painless Way to Change Your Eating Habits and Stay Gorgeously Thin All Your Life

First, you have to find out what foods make you fat. Sit down now and study any one of dozens of paperbacks which list the calorie count for all foods. You can even find books which list foods by brand names. You're sure to find many surprises about the things you eat, some good, some bad.

(The books will tell you how many calories you can afford, based on your bone structure and height. Speaking very generally, you probably won't gain weight on 1,500 calories a day. If you are especially active you might even stretch this to 2,000. You will *certainly* lose pounds and fat inches over a period of time if you cut your daily caloric intake below 1,200.)

Secondly, keep a scale in your room. Weigh yourself without clothes every morning. This is for morale purposes: you weigh less in the morning than at evening, because the body is like a fire which consumes fuel even as you sleep. Don't confuse yourself by weighing on other scales at other times, with your clothes on. It will also help if you will keep a daily record of your weight.

Thirdly, don't go on any crash diets. Or fad diets.

That's right, no major diet trauma. All-out diets frustrate you too much and leave you unhappy and ill-tempered. Losing weight isn't all *that* important, you decide; and you fall off the diet with a lovely caloric orgy. That's a defeat. The world may not care much, but you do. At this stage in your life you don't want to build up *any* history of failing, at anything.

Accept the fact that as a young, energetic person you don't have to cut down on food intake very much. But you have to cut down a little all the time. Nobody wants to think about dieting every waking moment of her life—it's too boring. So, decide now to eliminate certain foods and eating situations forever. Yes: a life decision right now so you don't have to think about it any more.

Painless Plan A: No "Automatic" Snacking

✳ Most people who are overweight eat all the time; sometimes they aren't even aware they are doing it. Don't let this happen to you. Ask yourself (a) Am I hungry? or (b) Will this snack really mean anything to me—will I feel *deprived* if I don't eat it?

✳ One good way to approach it is to decide that you are only going to do "social" eating. In Alcoholics Anonymous they say that as soon as you have to drink even when there is no one around, you may be on your way. What if you resolved that you would only eat when you have someone to eat *with?*

✳ At the very least, make up your mind never to take food or drink to your room.

✳ Or to the TV set. If you have to get up and walk for it, there is a fair chance you can postpone or eliminate some of the between-meal snacking you are doing. If you can agree that in our house all food has to be eaten in the kitchen or dining room, and it has to be eaten *with* somebody, you will cut hundreds of calories a day without too much strain.

Painless Plan B: One Treat Is Enough

✳ I've watched you eat a dessert at dinner, then rummage in the kitchen for a handful of cookies, and a half hour later scoop out a dish of ice cream to take to the TV set. I don't say you have to cut out dessert, but make up your mind that one dessert at a time is enough. It has to be another entire eating occasion before you can have another treat. Again, this is not such a sacrifice. All you are giving up is the grossest of over-indulgence.

❄ The word "treat" should be construed narrowly. For example, if you have ordered a beautiful box of hot buttered popcorn at the movies, that's treat enough. You don't add a candy bar to it, because that's *two* treats at the same time. And of course you have a diet soda with the popcorn, or you simply go to the theatre drinking fountain. Tough? Come on.

❄ Another example. At our local ice cream emporium they have something for three dollars called a "Pig's Dinner." It's actually served in a wooden trough. You do understand that you *can't* have one of these any more? Not even an ordinary banana split or hot fudge sundae with whipped cream, nuts, and cherry, either. Just ask for an ice cream cone—your favorite flavor. *Not* two dips. Just one treat at a time. Spend as long as possible licking your cone down to satisfaction, telling yourself the whole time that isn't it lucky you can be on a diet and still have an ice cream cone any time you want it.

Painless Plan C: What Foods Can You Give Up?

❄ What about bread? You eat so much bread when you go out (hamburgers, hot dogs, heroic sandwiches, grilled sandwiches, pizza, etc.), would it kill you if you resolved never to eat any bread when you are at home? You don't need sandwiches at home. You can put the ingredients on a plate and eat them. Or nibble a salad. Remember, you're not getting much fruit, meat, and vegetables when you eat out. You've got to have some of these; so concentrate on them at home and cut out the bread.

❄ Could you resolve to ban potatoes as a lifetime thing? I love potatoes, and they're not the worst caloric food in the world by themselves. But after you add milk and mash them and then ladle on some gravy, or add sour cream or butter to baked potatoes, or fry them in deep fat and then add ketchup, well, you've got a pretty potent pile of calories.

❀ Check your calorie counter. What other significant foods can you bear to give up permanently? Don't be like Huck Finn at Lent: he gave up persimmons, which he didn't much like anyway.

PAINLESS PLAN D: "MISS GARBAGE PAIL"

❀ You never take *seconds* of anything. No matter how hard they beg you.

❀ You plan to *throw away* a third of whatever is on your plate. The fact is many, many Americans eat more than they need. We just don't do enough with our bodies to burn up all the food we take in. It's not easy to refuse food, especially if it's good and exactly what you wanted. But at some point in the meal comes a diminished return. If the latest bite really isn't all that great, why not leave it there for a while and think about it? Get busy talking with family or friends.

Then when you look at it again think of yourself as a slob who cleans up her plate every time. Can you fantasy yourself being crowned "Miss Garbage Pail" as the crowd cheers, and then zoom in to notice that the faces in the crowd look suspiciously like hogs? Can you think of yourself as a hound dog licking your plate clean? And everybody else's plate too? Find some *horrid* image which will help to remind you that the last third is more than you need, or want.

❀ Practice throwing away a third of your junk food—*not* just the good nourishing family meals.

PAINLESS PLAN E: DAILY EXERCISE

You are probably under the impression that you have to run something like fifteen miles to lose a pound and therefore exercise is futile. New evidence, however, is shaping up which indicates that this isn't so at all. Entirely aside from this, researchers have discovered you may need daily exercise to make your body metabolize its food at the maximum rate for successful dieting, even if the exercise itself doesn't consume the calories.

One Harvard research group took twenty-eight overweight high school girls and matched them with a slim group by age, height, and cultural status. Although the fat girls ate less food—several hundred calories per day less—they gained weight. Everyone was ready to write this off as simply a glandular problem when it was discovered that the fat girls got only *one-third as much exercise*.

This was the beginning of the "metabolic trigger" theory. When you get sufficient exercise the trigger is pulled and the caloric intake is better utilized in daily functioning, rather than being stored as fat.

What kind of exercise should you do, and how much of it? Certainly serious swimming (as opposed to standing around in the shallow end of the pool) will qualify. And a set of tennis where you actually have to *run* will do your figure no harm. You can think of a dozen activities that are fun—ask your boy friend what sports he likes and then share some of them.

No matter what the theory, some kind of vigorous physical activity every day has got to be good for your body—and probably your soul too.

This is not really a diet but a return to a more normal, natural way of living, to a time when we didn't have so many goodies constantly at our disposal. Few people can practice self-discipline even in small measure. If you can stay slim because you habitually resist a dozen daily minor temptations, then you will have done more than keep your figure. You will have learned something about character.

13 ✳

Let's Not Think About Sex

It *is* almost unthinkable, isn't it? These naïve, half-grown, unaware, foolish-headed *babies* blundering around with the great mystery of life? No, no, not my kids, we mutter; maybe next year, but surely not now. Maybe even two years from now. Maybe they're slow developers. Maybe they'll discover a new fad: virginity might stage a comeback. My kids having sex? Listen, I've got enough trouble without worrying about *that*.

But of course we do worry. A primeval fear surges right out of the unconscious into the daily decisions of every parent. Just as we guard a toddler against running out into the street, so we attempt to mount vigil against our children's premature sexual experimentation in their teen years—especially our daughters. As modern and rational as we may be, we are all saddled with the taboo of a thousand generations which says that sex shouldn't happen until society formally grants permission and legal responsibilities are assigned and accepted.

We expect our children to ignore sex for ten or even fifteen years past puberty while they get their education, start their careers, adjust themselves to their role in society, and begin to earn a middle-class living. But in our hearts we feel this is monstrously unnatural, and we know that our sons and daughters can't and *won't* wait that long. We really don't want them to.

God knows our generation tried to wait. From the vantage point of middle age we may even congratulate ourselves on the way we preserved the surface amenities. But how many of us are truly satisfied with the development of our sensual capacities? When we examine our sex lives, just how proud are we of our hangups? From the Kinsey reports through Masters and Johnson to the latest magazine polls we see the dismal statistics of frustration, distortion, fear, and failure. Our generation may have done better than our Victorian parents, but that's not saying much.

Who are we, really, to teach our children happiness in sex? To say how and when and with whom it ought to be, and just how it all ought to be connected up with love? The only answer we have is *wait*. But there are some areas of life in which less is not necessarily more. And "later" is sometimes too late.

Fortunately, this issue does not lie within our direct control. No matter how close we are to our kids we can never know much, if anything, about their sexual lives—any more than our parents knew about us. We have only one way to help our children, by pushing them as fast as we can toward emotional adulthood. Many people disagree. Yes, yes, they say, that's fine about growing up and accepting responsibility, but our children are just starting to find themselves at eighteen. College graduation is soon enough to expect them to be fully mature.

But the sexual question can't wait that long. Teenagers today have to face up to it when they are fourteen, fifteen, sixteen, and seventeen. We're kidding ourselves if we say they aren't making decisions about this while they are still living under our roof. We all know the tyranny of peer-group conformity. Just how well equipped are our kids to resist the phrase "everybody else is doing it"? It's one thing to let them go along with clothes and hair-style fads—these issues often are not worth debating. But as parents we have seen a hundred more important areas in which they either give in and conform or they are aware enough of their own strength to make an individual decision. Every parent with an early deadline is looking for opportunities to lead a child into independent thinking—*before* the sex or drug problem reaches crisis dimensions.

In our time all peer-group pressure was used to support the idea of chastity for "nice girls." Even the boys believed in it. In high school my gang and I had a Model A Ford called the *Mayflower*. Our slogan was that "many a girl has come across in this boat"; but in fact none ever did. We necked for hours, but we "respected" them too much even to try, seriously. There were two or three girls in school reputed to be "wild," and all our sexual fantasies shifted to them.

Today, of course, peer pressure pushes toward all-out sex for everybody. A girl is accused of not being "loving" or "giving" if she is unwilling to release the sexual head of steam she has created in her boy friend. Above all, she is taunted with being a baby if she fears to venture into the ultimate sensual unknown. In some high schools to have a confirmed sexual affair is almost a rite of passage.

Boys, too, are often pushed into these affairs before they are ready, simply because there *is* a girl available and eager to prove herself. If your child and mine have not had considerable experience (and success) in resisting peer pressure before this decision comes up, they are not going to fare well.

It's not just a mechanical, intellectual decision process, of course. The foundation of *all* moral courage is emotional security. If our children have a bedrock feeling that they are not only loved but respected in the family, they don't *have* to let the outside world taunt them into anything. They can afford to suffer a little derision, a few social cuts, even the mild limbo of being singled out as a "square."

Hence the urgency for both mother and father to display love on a daily basis and to reduce the confrontation level to the point where it does not neutralize or destroy this parental proof of love. Every human psyche requires a sanctuary; if your child doesn't have it at home—if he feels constantly attacked in every part of his being—he is going to seek relief wherever he can find it. Thus the drift into drugs and sex.

Parents must also take positive steps to teach their children the essence of making friends outside the home. The cutting edge of peer pressure is the fear of being left out. But if a child early learns the basics of human relations, if he learns how to *have* a friend or two, this too is a security to fall back upon when he wants to resist the demands of the mob. Sometimes it takes two friends, reinforcing each other's courage, to stick by an honest and valid decision. And these two friends don't always have to be of the same sex.

How do you help a child to understand the nature of friendship? In the early teen years you simply have to be *close* enough to offer a little judicious counseling—close enough emotionally so the child will talk to you but also close enough physically so that you can *see* what is beginning to happen with an incipient friendship. The best way this can happen is for your kids to bring their friends home. If your home isn't one of the most attractive places they can meet their friends, you aren't likely to get the chance to help.

Now, "attractive" doesn't mean rich and fancy. It means that you always make the visitors feel welcome, and then the kids have a private place to go where they know you will leave them alone. We have eight rooms in our house, and they're all in use; but down in the basement they have a private place. The laundry area is screened off, and there are bright lights for Ping-Pong and dim lights for playing records. In the corner is a queen-size waterbed with big pillows and an old black-and-white TV set which miraculously still works. We didn't plan to buy a waterbed; the kids talked us into it years earlier when they were still having neighborhood pals in for sleep-overs.

Privacy and respect are the keys to whether teenagers will consistently be willing to meet under your roof. If your child is entertaining a friend in his room with the door closed you can't burst in without knocking. Similarly, we have never charged down the basement stairs without considerable advance notice. When our children have guests in the basement, we make a point of not going down for our own errands if these can possibly be postponed; and if we have to call down to ask them to lower the decibel level on the stereo we try to do so politely.

Teens can't stay in one place for long, and so you get to talk to their friends in neutral meeting grounds such as the kitchen. I don't do much of the cooking in our family, but I do make great popcorn in an old aluminum pan; the sound and aroma of popping corn always draws a crowd from all parts of the house. Sometimes we migrate together to the family TV set, sometimes we just sit around eating in the kitchen, or sometimes the kids and their friends take a big wooden bowl of my popcorn and retreat to the basement. This is the nice balance of contact and escape which all young people seek—and it *has* to be entirely at their control.

Occasionally we're invited down to the basement to play Ping-Pong doubles, and we always accept even if it wasn't exactly what we had in mind to do at that moment. Sometimes we invite kids and friends to join us at the family TV set if the program is something they are likely to be especially interested in. We don't feel hurt if they decline. Fathers, weary and seeking a little solitude after a tough day at work, often tend to ignore this homely ebb and flow within the house. But it's just in the casual routine, rather than in the crisis moments, that the opening comes. For example, mothers are traditionally chief etiquette advisers to both sexes on the first tentative dating problems; but when you stop to think about it, Dad has been there too, and he may have something valuable to offer if he is "available" to the situation. When the kids reach eighteen there isn't much you dare say to them about relationships between the sexes, but at thirteen and fourteen both a daughter and son will gladly accept all the help they can get.

I still remember Eve's first date. Mark had visited the house several times; although he was several years older, we liked him immediately and told Eve so. She seemed pleased that we had confirmed her judgment. (Can you remember your own first boy or girl friend—how *unsure* you were?) One Friday night he asked her for a formal date: he'd like to take her out to lunch the next day. Not just old Burger King but Charlie Brown's, a fancy college-age dating place in our town where the lights are low and the burgers go for $1.75 each.

I heard her on the phone asking him what she should wear; he didn't seem to know, but Marion did. That Saturday noon I passed Eve's door and saw her sitting on her bed all dressed up and waiting. I told her how nice she looked and sat down beside her. "Should I take some money?" she asked.

"A girl always ought to carry some cash for emergencies," I said. "Who's going to pay the check, anyway?"

"I don't know," she answered with some surprise.

"Well, if you have dessert the bill could easily come to six dollars, with tip. And since you have all those baby-sitting jobs maybe you can afford it better than Mark."

"What should I do?" she asked eagerly.

"When I was in high school the boy always had to pay—no question about it. But times are different now. A girl is independent and if she can pay her own way she should. Let me tell you how Lisa handles it. When waitress gives the boy the check she says, quite casually, 'Let me share this with you.' If he's old-fashioned and insists on paying it, she doesn't make a fuss. She just says, 'All right, but next time let me take *you* to lunch, OK?' And the boys generally agree to that."

Eve looked genuinely relieved at this solution. Much later I heard indirectly that the lunch had come off very well, and from that time on Mark had been very pleased indeed that *his* girl always paid her own way. A women's lib lesson for two.

This was a small incident, surely, only one of dozens, perhaps hundreds, that I no longer remember. When both father and mother can maintain contact, each in his own way, the parents together begin to gain confidence that their kids are going to make it all right as they move out into the world. And this confidence is catching—the kids begin to believe it too.

Yes, yes, obviously all parents are in favor of more contact with their teenagers—if they can manage it. But am I saying that parents and children can never really face the issue of sex head-on? What about explaining the "facts of life," for example?

I had a talk with Lisa once, when she was thirteen and already budding into a very attractive young woman. The conventional wisdom is that Freudian fears and desires taboo this subject between

fathers and daughters, and mothers and sons. Of course Freud himself was a Victorian and lived in an era when any verbalization about
sex was in itself a titillation, if not a downright excitation. Today,
however, all of us have been so deluged with information and discussion in the public print that the subject becomes rather ho-hum. The
actual mechanics of reproduction are known to most children these
days. One evening our family had the privilege of observing our cat
give birth to four kittens right next to the couch where we sat watching a movie on TV. Another time we all watched a British documen-
tary about farmers which showed in great detail how the stallion
bred a mare, followed by an incredible sequence in which the
farmer, his sons, and the vet sweated mightily to deliver a foal which
apparently had been poorly positioned within the womb. Our children were not horrified or even shocked by all this—merely fascinated and involved.

Nevertheless, I wanted to talk to Lisa directly about sex in
humankind. If I was prepared to teach all the rest of the stormy
geography in the sea of life, why should sex remain an uncharted
island? Maybe I could give her something those fifth-grade Kotex
films in school hadn't covered, or clear up confusion in a few areas
that I knew Marion had been too delicate to open up. In any case I
could tell her frankly how many young men feel about sex. So we sat
down together, just the two of us alone in the house one quiet
Sunday afternoon.

Very dispassionately I launched into puberty in the female and
the male, what actually happens in the act of intercourse, the development of the fetus in pregnancy, and the history of abortion in
this country, including the very confused legal position today. I
discussed masturbation and venereal disease and homosexuality, and
then spent quite a long time on the role of emotion and love in sex.
Lisa listened attentively, but I could not really provoke any questions. I concluded by listing the various methods of contraception.

"You forgot one," she said.

"What?"

"Condoms."

"You know about them?"

"Sure, we had all this in health class. You just walk into the drugstore and ask for them. The boy has a responsibility in not getting the girl pregnant too, you know."

I tried not to let her see the conflicting emotions which raged in me. "You're quite right. I'm glad to see they teach that."

"Oh, they're very big on that," Lisa answered brightly. "Anything else?"

"I don't know. Is there? You seem to know more about this than I do."

She leaned over and gave me a kiss on the forehead. "Thank you, Daddy," she said. Our conversation broke up with, I think, a little disappointment on both sides: on her part because I hadn't had anything new or sensational to say, and for me because I had thought I would be providing a signal service to her in opening up the real world. There is such a thing as *vanity* in parenthood. I reflected later. Still, I suppose she gave me good marks for the effort, and it did prove that we could discuss sex in a calm and reasonable way if the need ever arose.

Wow, at thirteen. I keep telling myself that future shock is here, and our kids may be coping better than we are. Do you know what the schools are teaching your children about sex? I discovered that in our system they don't have any textbooks on this subject or any homework which might alarm parents who haven't quite moved into the twentieth century. The more I thought about it, the more I liked the idea that all the kids in our town were getting this information as a matter of course, just as they were learning algebra, English, and foreign languages. And I was pleased that apparently a very considerable effort had been made to link sex with morality, love, and responsibility.

How had it all come about? Like most towns we'd had a teenage drug scare a few years ago. The parents had come down hard that the schools had to do something . . . teach the dangers of drugs— and do it at an age before the kids were likely to get hooked. The parents never mentioned anything about sex, of course; nobody wants to raise *that* cloud of fear, shame, and hangup in public. And yet if you are a teacher and you are plunging right into the heart of the teen lifestyle, talking about what can happen when you start hallucinating or main-lining, it must seem sheer hypocrisy not to go on to sex, pregnancy, abortion, and contraception.

Education is very trendy these days, however, so five years later when Eve had reached thirteen and Eric fourteen, I wasn't completely sure their health class was still putting out the same information. I asked them about sex education but couldn't get a clear answer from either. After a little searching, I found a book * which in just the opening chapter explained most of what they really needed to know. It was designed for high school girls but serves equally well for boys. It also contains the simplest and clearest sketches of the male and female sex organs and their functioning that I have ever seen.

I gave the book to my son and daughter and then separately went through the chapter with each of them. Yes, they had already learned it all, I was relieved to discover, and so my input dealt chiefly with the relationship of love to sex. My comments were the same for Eric as for Eve, and both listened attentively and with acceptance. I recommend this book, or something similar, as a painless way of checking out what your kids know, and as a natural lead-in to whatever moral issues you want to raise on this subject.

Perhaps it's just as well that sex is a strictly private matter for our children. No matter how rational we are, few parents are equipped to cope with the concrete image of a son or daughter in the act of love. Sometimes we can't bear to think about it even after they get married, and certainly not while they are still in their teens. Let me tell you about the one time the curtain parted for just an

---

* *Other Choices for Becoming a Woman*, Joyce Slayton Mitchell, ed. (Know, Inc., Box 86031, Pittsburgh, Pa. 15221). The opening chapter, "Learning About Sex," is written by Dr. Mary Jane Gray, professor of obstetrics and gynecology at the University of Vermont. The second chapter, which deals with teen friendships, is written by Margaret Mead.

instant—or I thought it had. I'm sorry to say I acted rather badly. Lisa was sixteen and a half and her friend, Johnny, was eighteen. They had been going together for about eighteen months. We didn't exactly approve of the institution of "going steady," any more than our own parents had, but given the way it developed there wasn't much we could do about it. Anyway we liked Johnny as a human being and thought he was very good for Lisa in many respects, and she for him. Earlier she'd had a few casual boy friends but Johnny was her first love; we were sympathetic because it became apparent that Lisa was also his first true girl friend, and he was certainly not ahead of her in emotional development or worldly sophistication.

We naturally supposed that the relationship would break up after a few months, but they were so helpful and supportive to each other in working through many of the traumas of teen life that we saw they had moved beyond the boy-girl stage to become classic friends—surely the closest friend each one had ever had. What can parents do in a case like this except try to be glad?

"My God," Marion said to me one night, "they spend *all* their time together. Apparently there isn't anything they keep secret or don't share. It's like a mini-marriage."

"Let's hope it isn't quite that," I answered gloomily.

"Well, if it isn't already, they can't resist forever. They're only human. What are we going to do?"

"Watch the papers for a sale on chastity belts."

"She's too young to get this deeply involved. Good lord, she's only sixteen!"

"Yes, but she's more mature, a better-balanced person than either you or I were at sixteen. Can you remember?"

"Yes, she certainly is. But we still can't just sit by and watch it happen."

"We don't know that anything is happening or going to happen. Anyway, he'll be gone the whole summer as a camp counselor and that may wind it up, or at least cool things off."

"Let's hope so. I feel so worried and frustrated."

"Like every other parent in the world."

Not long afterward Marion left to visit relatives for a few days and took the younger children with her, leaving Lisa and me to manage alone. My daughter was totally preoccupied with Johnny. On the last Saturday before he was to leave for camp they drove off early in the morning to spend the day in a state park twenty miles away and didn't return until 11:30 P.M. Johnny came in to say goodbye briefly; he seemed a bit ill at ease as he shook my hand, but I gave it no thought at the time.

I was about to start a good old movie classic on TV and asked her to join me, but she said she was exhausted and going straight to bed. I accepted this with a small pang of disappointment; oh well, Johnny would be gone tomorrow and then maybe we'd have a chance to do something together. I suppose I was vaguely aware of some resentment that a young man had totally preempted my daughter for the past year and a half.

Five minutes later she came down in her best nightgown. "I'm going to sleep on the waterbed tonight, Dad," she said. "It's so hot upstairs and that air conditioner isn't working too well."

"Oh? Want me to go up and look at it?"

"No, no, I'd rather sleep downstairs. That waterbed is really cool on a night like this. Somehow the motion of it makes you sleep better when you're really tired, too."

I accepted this with a "good night," although something in the back of my mind marked it down as rather odd. Lisa loved her room and had never slept in the basement on the waterbed except when she had a girl friend staying over. Still, the air conditioner *was* getting old. Back to the movie.

Every householder has an ear for the distinctive noises of his citadel, and a few minutes later, despite the sound on the TV screen, I thought I heard the creak of our side screen door opening—the door that leads directly to the basement. I watched the end of the movie scene and then walked out to the kitchen to check the door. It was unlocked. I was sure I had locked it.

"Lisa?" I called down to the basement.

"What?" she answered sleepily.

"Oh, sorry. I thought I heard you go out."

"No."

"Oh. Well, good night again."

I walked slowly back to the TV set, my head in the kind of Dr. Jekyll–Mr. Hyde turmoil that every parent has experienced. Reason warred with fear and suspicion—love, anger, and frustration all mixed up together. The internal dialogue went something like this:

HYDE: You know damn well you locked that door.

JEKYLL: No, I don't remember for sure.

HYDE: You know you heard the screen door open.

JEKYLL: I'm not positive.

HYDE: If she didn't go out, then somebody came in. And you know who!

JEKYLL: Why would they want to do that? They spent all day together.

HYDE: Who knows anything about kids? He's down there on that waterbed with her. In the "Passion Pit." Remember when you gave it that name? Funny man!

JEKYLL: I don't believe any of this.

HYDE: Of course you do. You saw him when he shook your hand goodbye tonight. The reason he couldn't look you in the eye was because he knew he was coming back. He was going to sneak in and sleep with your daughter under your own roof.

JEKYLL: You make it sound like I'm a cuckold.

HYDE: That's about the way you feel, isn't it? Come on, let's go down and catch them in the act.

JEKYLL: What? You're *insane!*

HYDE: Well, at least let's go listen at the top of the stairs.

JEKYLL: That's as far as I'll go. (*They move to the top of the basement steps.*) See? Not a sound! This is nothing but your perverted imagination.

HYDE: Yeah? The little bitch lied to you, and you know it.

JEKYLL: Don't call her that! She's never lied to me—that I know of.

HYDE: OK, all-wise and loving father, let's go up to her room and see if that air conditioner works.

JEKYLL: No. We're going back and watch the rest of the movie.

HYDE: You mean you're going to stick your head in a pile of sand and pretend nothing is happening.

JEKYLL: That's right. I don't believe anything is happening. I don't believe he's down there, and I don't believe they're making love even if he is.

HYDE: Don't be naïve. She's in her nightgown. You know—

JEKYLL: Shut up and watch the movie!

HYDE (*after a time*): All right, you've been staring at that screen for five minutes and you haven't heard a damn word they said. I'm going down and check this out!

JEKYLL (*at the top of the stairs*): See, not a *sound*. I tell you, I'll kill you before I'll let you go down there and stage an ugly scene which might curdle our relationship for all time. Remember my mother? Remember one night when I was a senior in high school and came home to get some blankets so Jack and I could sleep out in the Boy Scout cabin? She was convinced that we had a couple of girls in the car and she absolutely shocked Jack by the things she said. We were totally innocent at the time—didn't even know any girls who would go out to a cabin with us. But she wouldn't believe us! And *you* never really forgave her for the humiliation of that scene.

HYDE: Yeah, but your sweet daughter really *does* have a boy in the basement. . . At the very least you could check the street out in front to see if his father's car is there.

JEKYLL (*peering out the front door*): See, no car.

HYDE: He probably rode his bicycle. It's parked at the side of the house.

JEKYLL: I can't go out there in my pajamas and bare feet.

HYDE (*exiting*): Why not, it's a warm night.

JEKYLL (*in the driveway*): I don't see any bicycle. *Ow!* I stubbed my toe.

HYDE: He probably hid it up the street. If you stoop down you can look through that basement window and see them.

JEKYLL: I won't spy on my kids. My toe hurts! I can't believe I'm doing this—it's kind of an "I Love Lucy" farce.

HYDE: Just one peek. There's a faint light from the bathroom.

JEKYLL: No . . . well, just one peek. No, I don't see a damn thing. There *aren't* two bodies there. None of this is happening. Any second now the cops are going to come roaring up the street and arrest me in my pajamas for peeping into my own basement window. For God's sake, go in and go to bed—you imagined the whole thing.

HYDE: Oh yes? Look over there. Why is the screen door propped open? It wasn't that way when you first checked. She propped it open for him because she knows it squeaks. Convinced?

JEKYLL (*groan*): I guess so. Let's go in and think this over.

HYDE (*back in front of the TV set*): You can't really let her get away with it, you know.

JEKYLL: Why not? I got away with *lots* of things when I was a kid and it didn't kill me. If you hadn't had such a damned suspicious mind, we never would have found out.

HYDE: So you approve of them down there making love, under your own roof.

JEKYLL: Well, it's her roof too.

HYDE: You're evading.

JEKYLL: Look, they were up in that state park for something like fourteen hours today. Flying kites and swimming and reading poetry to each other, they said. That park is big enough and isolated enough so that if they wanted to make love they could have done it—some leafy glen maybe, with the sun filtering through the leaves. Very romantic. So what's going on downstairs is nothing new. It's a kind of goodbye—because at their age a whole summer of separation seems like a lifetime.

HYDE: You can't control what happens away from home, but you have a moral obligation to see that it doesn't happen right here under your nose. In effect, she's flaunting it.

JEKYLL: No, she isn't. She tried to cover it. Neither one of them is a very good liar, that's all.

HYDE: I think you ought to get him the hell out of the house before he gets her pregnant.

JEKYLL: My God, what a primitive ape! First of all, just because he's down there doesn't mean they are making love. And secondly, what if they are? I'd feel more comfortable if she were eighteen or twenty or twenty-three, because then I'd be more confident that she was psychologically ready to handle it, but she's a very mature girl for her age. Maybe she *is* ready. Anything they do together is certainly done with great love and tenderness and consideration, and they are responsible kids too. Maybe this is the best time it could happen for her—except I don't believe it *is* happening.

HYDE: It's not like you to back away from a problem. You damn well better go down there and settle this.

JEKYLL: How? Bust down there with a shotgun and threaten to blow his head off? What in hell can I possibly say to them? This is her private life, and anything I can do to influence it I've either already done or not done. (*Jekyll snaps off the TV set.*)

HYDE: I can see you're going to give up.

JEKYLL: That's right. I'm going to feed you a tranquilizer, and I'm going to bed.

Well, that was years ago. As I was reading the proofs for this book one day recently, Lisa happened to be home. "Listen," I said, "I can't stand it any longer. I've got to ask you something. You don't have to answer, but let me ask anyway. Remember when you were sixteen that last day before Johnny went off to camp? You went up to the state park and then came home and slept on the waterbed that night?"

She had to think about it. "Oh yes, I remember."

"Johnny really *was* down there that night, wasn't he?"

"Yes. We'd had such a marvelous day that we couldn't bear to give it up. So I told him to come back and we'd spend the whole night together. Very romantic, you know? We were really in love."

"Were you aware that I had some idea he was there?"

"Of course. He only stayed a couple of minutes. We decided that if you were up-tight he ought to just go home."

I thought about confessing to her that I had peeped in the basement window, but in the end I couldn't bear to.

"Nothing would have happened, you know," Lisa said. "We would have slept in each other's arms, like all those Shelley poems. We never had sex together. We'd made a decision that we weren't ready for it, and we stuck to it."

"You mean, in all that time—"

"That's right. That's what you parents were preaching, wasn't it? Responsibility? You've got to have confidence in your kids, Dad."

It took me a few seconds to recover. "I almost always did, honey," I said. "Except maybe once."

14 ✳

Letting Them Fail—
But Not for Too Long

We say we want our children to learn about Life, but we really can't bear for them to face unpleasant consequences. We not only don't want them to suffer, we are so shamelessly protective that we don't even want them to experience *disappointment*—if it can be avoided. Let me confess the Battle of the Bike Lock:

Many years ago in the city I lost a bicycle in just the minute or so it took me to walk into a standup pizza parlor and eat one slice. Since the bike was leaning against the store window in full view not fifteen feet away, I hadn't locked it. I kicked myself all the way home, and I'm still furious.

When Eve was small she dropped her shiny new Huffy—the training wheels just removed—on the front lawn. I saw it when I drove up the driveway late that night, but forgot to go back and pick it up. The next morning it was gone.

One spring when Lisa was fifteen she left her bicycle at a friend's house and, despite our urging, refused for many days to retrieve it. The friend rode the bike to school, left it unlocked, and it was stolen.

So, by the time Eric received his new imported ten-speed bike for Christmas several years ago, I was a bit paranoid about theft. A few months later I began to notice that while my son put his bicycle in the garage he usually "forgot" to lock it with the strong chain I had bought him. And our garage—really not much more than a shed— had no doors.

Three stolen bikes is enough for one family! I howled. He smiled, and "forgot" again. For months I nagged him and sent him out late at night to put the chain around his bicycle. Didn't he like his bike? I asked. Was he deliberately trying to lose it? No, no, he insisted, and forgot again. Twice I put his bicycle in the basement and set him afoot for a week. Repentance was short.

Then—trouble!—one Saturday night the boy right across the street lost his new $140 bike out of his garage. That ought to do it, I thought—*that* ought to strike home. But just two nights later Eric's bike was unlocked again.

I warned him that if his bicycle was stolen he'd have to earn the money to replace it. He said he understood. But it still bugged me to see him go on taking this risk. Why did I care so much? I didn't want him to experience that terrible sense of loss; to a boy a bike is often more like a friend and companion than a simple machine. I didn't want him to be angry, to walk to school cursing himself for his stupidity. Why couldn't he learn from my lesson, from the total family experience, that this is not an era when you can leave a valuable piece of property casually unprotected?

Are there parents out there smiling at my naïve attempt to teach a middle-class teenager that property is worth caring for? Why should they care? Property has always flowed to them automatically, and if for some reason it disappears then other goodies just like it, or better, will appear in its place—by magic.

I saw Eric one day at the shopping center and his bike was carefully locked; he said he also locked it at school. Thus it dawned on me at last that it was only at home—where I could notice—that my son "forgot." I doubt if Eric was consciously aware of the message he was sending me. We had been engaged in a battle of wills. I thought we had been fighting about the principle of protecting property; apparently he thought we had been fighting about my right to dictate this small detail in his life.

Ah woe, parents and children never seem to contest on common ground. Obviously Eric was right: this lesson was not mine to teach. We had agreed that *he* would have the sweat of earning a replacement, and the inconvenience of losing his wheels while he did it. The loss would be his alone. So why was I interfering? Maybe the lesson now would be a very good thing—saving him greater pain later on. But damn it, I thought, why does he have to learn in such a dumb and avoidable way?

In fact, he hasn't. Two years later the bike is still unlocked and—miraculously—still untouched. I'm glad for my son. Every time I look at it I tell myself Father Doesn't Necessarily Know Best or, even if he does, sometimes he's better off keeping his mouth shut.

Breaking the Spell of Defeat

Occasionally parents run into a series of rebuffs in quick succession. After encountering what seems like a stone wall of resistance we often throw up our hands and say, hell, I've got my own life to lead and maybe the kids just have to go through the same hard knocks I did. We decide to leave them alone. But it's one thing to grant our teens the right to make a mistake when the consequences are not serious (and a learning experience can result). It's quite another matter to stand by and let our offspring slide into one failure after another in areas which seriously involve their self-worth. If we expect them to become fully functioning adults at eighteen, they have to arrive there believing they are winners in life, not losers.

When an unpleasant event occurs in a child's life he assigns blame. At first it is always someone else's fault. If he loses in a game with his friends, for example, a young child often accuses the victor of "cheating." As he moves into his teen years, however, this ego defense no longer functions so well. Sheer weight of observation forces him to concede that nobody cheated; he simply lost, or failed. If he fails repeatedly at something he thinks is important, he becomes very angry at himself. Self-blame is cancerous: if allowed to fester too long it spreads to other parts of the psyche, and soon the young person no longer remembers the specifics of failure. He just feels generally no damn good in all areas.

W. Timothy Gallwey is a tennis teacher who talks about this phenomenon in an interesting book called *The Inner Game of Tennis.* Gallwey suggests that tennis is a microcosm of life itself, in that all of our psychological problems are acted out in dramatized and accelerated form. Events take place in an hour on a tennis court which in real life might unfold over the course of days, weeks, or months; nevertheless, they are real.

Let me tell you about a doubles match I played not so long ago. One of our regular tennis foursome was out of town, so another member brought along his son to fill in. Jack, who was home from college on vacation, is a brilliant student and something of an athlete. As we were warming up I watched his beautiful ground strokes and flashing overhead and thought: "Boy, he's going to dominate this game." Craftily, I arranged to get him as my partner for the first set.

Sure enough, we zipped through the first four games easily. But then something happened. Jack, trying to be too dazzling, double-faulted his serve away, and eventually we lost the set in a tie-breaker. Since we normally change partners after every set, Jack played with his father next. They lost. Then, playing with our third man, he lost again—badly. By this time Jack was not only cursing and muttering orders to himself but was angrily kicking balls out of his way, and once he even hurled his racket into the net.

His father never said a word; what *could* he say to a grown son? What could any of us say? I knew we were all aching to go up to him and say, "Jack, stop being so angry at yourself—it's only a friendly game. We like you, and we're impressed with your ability to hit a tennis ball. Stop making yourself so unhappy and spoiling the after-noon for us." Yet there was no way we could communicate this common sense to Jack without offending him. He was caught up in a hypnotic spell of self-blame. As we get older we permit ourselves to forgive some of our failures, but young people are merciless.

By the fourth and final set it was clear that Jack was not going to be able to break the spell himself—he was getting angrier. Since I was his partner again I decided, what the hell, why not me? We were losing 2–4, and as Jack was about to serve I called a conference back on the baseline. "Let's try something different," I said. "You've got a great deep spin serve. Draw him wide and protect my back-hand, OK?"

It worked perfectly. *Zip, boom, and the point!* Jack nodded in pleased surprise, then signaled that he was going to try a widely angled serve to our other opponent's backhand. We put that away, too. Suddenly we were talking and laughing and I was setting up some winners for him. Jack eased up and those beautiful low ground strokes were now going in, just as they had in the warm-up. We swept through the rest of the set without losing a game.

"Thank God," Jack said as we walked off the court. "I didn't think I'd ever get it together."

Neither Jack nor the other players were aware of the release mechanism. I think Jack had reached the point in his chain of nega-tive assumptions where he was not only doubting his ability as a tennis player but his worth as a human being. He had, in fact, regressed to childhood and was acting out all his unconscious memories of inadequacy and frustration and failure. I could not have broken his spell simply by saying, "Hey, Jack, shape up. Act your age and stop throwing a fit over a game that doesn't mean anything." This would have been further outside confirmation that every name he was calling himself was true, that he was acting in a dumb way, because he was a dumb person.

I broke into his spell not with words but with action, by re-sponding to him as a friend, a partner, and by offering a serious tactical proposal to engage his attention. The serve was something he could unquestionably deliver, and the rest was up to me. It was a way, suddenly, for Jack to think objectively about the game rather than about himself and his faults. But more than that, it was the breaking in on the *loneliness* of the self-hater. I reminded him that he was not alone, but part of a team. He had a partner who shared his fate, a partner who was not angry because things were going badly but who had a practical suggestion; and moreover was assuming part of the responsibility for the tactic's success.

Yes, under the concept of Adult at Eighteen we have to push our children to do everything themselves, and sometimes they can only learn by failing. But enough is enough. We cannot allow what happened to Jack in a tennis game to happen to our children in real life—not often, anyway. The teen ego is a rather jerry-built structure which has to be reinforced wherever possible; if even one leg of it seems in danger parents simply must intervene. We can't take over, but we can remind the teenager that he is not alone, that somebody is eternally watching and, in extremis, is ready to help.

We know as adults that we often wander down blind alleys. We go so far, and put so much emotional investment into our direction that we can't see where we are or why we are stymied. It then falls to a wife or husband or adult friend to say: Look, it was just a *bad idea*, cut your losses, back up, start over, and here's a new way to go. If this happens to us as adults, how much more often does it happen to our teenage children?

Perhaps it's a serious school problem and we have to intervene to get outside help, or give them our blessing to drop a course and try another, or maybe we even have to help them to transfer to a new school. Sometimes it's a work experience that for a variety of reasons just isn't right for them. Or some kind of over-idealized goal in the arts or repeated failure in a chosen sport. Or it's a complex of psychological problems, and we have to have the courage to seek professional advice or treatment.

It seems to me the rule of thumb is fairly obvious: if a teen can learn a lesson by failing, and the consequences are not great, then let him go his way. But if he's *already* learned all that he's going to learn in this particular chain of events, and if the pattern of defeat is likely to devastate him, then do whatever is necessary to see that his life isn't forever damaged before it's well begun.

The urgency inherent in the eighteenth-birthday deadline should help to keep us "tuned in" enough in these early years so that we recognize the difference between simple failure and looming disaster.

BULLETIN BOARD MESSAGE:
Nothing goes perfectly,
most of the time.

15 ❄

Dealing With Moods

The world is so full of glum and disappointed people that it's a tremendous relief to meet a smiling face, somebody who more often that not has something friendly to say, somebody who is not determined to lay his load upon you before you can tell him *your* troubles. Well, you might say, if you smile when all about you things are falling apart, maybe you're too dumb to realize what's happening. But in fact a "cheerful temperament" often results from a rational decision to overcome or work around problems rather than letting them dominate your mind-set.

I think we need to communicate this to our children. There is no reason we should tolerate kids who wake up grumpy because they have to get out of bed, and there is no reason we have to put up with teens who drift into sullenness because they can't think of any other way to hold their faces.

Young people today are particularly prone to what psychiatrist Karen Horney calls "neurotic claims"—the feeling that somehow *you*, adorable perfect you, should not be subject to the ordinary laws, rules, and petty annoyances of the workaday world. Broken promises, lost articles, pimples and cowlicks, schedule interruption, machines not working, other people's stupidity, even bad weather: why should all this happen to you? How can the world possibly be so screwed up?

We have to tell our kids that, yes, if things *can* go wrong, they will. But the question is: how upset are you going to be about this? All of us have our neurotic claims on life, but if we are in a bad mood most of the time, how much sympathy can we expect from family and friends? Yes, they should give us love and support when we need it, but how much can we demand of these people day after day? Their gift should be to help with *specific* problems; they should not be perpetually bogged down trying to jolly us out of generalized angers and despair.

One Saturday morning at brunch all I could see around me was glum or petulant faces. My attempts at communication were met with mumbles, if that. As far as I knew there wasn't any reason why three kids at the same time should be so depressed or angry, so I lost my cool. I stalked over to the kitchen blackboard and wrote in large letters:

SMILE, DAMN IT!
OR I'LL KILL YOU.

"That's dumb," Eric said.

"Why should we smile if we don't feel like it?" Eve said.

"We don't have to put on an act for you," Lisa added.

"No, you don't," I replied. As I looked at the words I had to laugh. "To tell you the truth, I really didn't know what I was trying to say when I wrote it. Obviously nobody has to smile to please other people, but on the other hand, when you are living closely together nobody has a right to poison the atmosphere, either. Unless there's a pretty good reason."

They were listening now. Every parent recognizes the hopeful signs when a teen's face improves from sullenness to profound disinterest. But sometimes it takes a Dramatic Gesture, like leaping out of your chair with a howl, before you can get this much attention. "Let me try to explain what I mean about poisoning the atmosphere," I said. "Somebody wakes up in a black mood. The first person he encounters is in a good—or at least neutral—mood and tries to make a normal friendly overture. But the second person gets rebuffed, sometimes brutally. Since he didn't do anything to earn this rejection he becomes angry. Often he can't get any satisfaction or even response from the first person, so, without realizing it, he turns this anger or aggression against a third person. Before you know it the whole family is annoyed with one another, and nobody quite knows why. This is a process that can go on with any group of people who live or work together, so I'm not just talking about our family relationships."

"People can't help how they *feel*," Eve said.

"I think we have to make an important distinction here," Marion said. "Families and friends exist to support one another. We don't have to put up a brave front if we have a problem or a need—we can ask for help. When we love someone we grant this help instinctively without question."

"It's all a matter of how you ask for the help, isn't it? If you snarl at somebody you can't expect him to understand what it is that you really want," I said. "Other people have their problems too. If they love you—especially your parents—they will put aside their own problems for a while to help you. But you have to let them help you."

"What if you just plain feel *bad*, and you don't know why?" Lisa asked.

"Put a sticker on your forehead that says 'Feeling Mean Today,' " Eric said.

"That's not a bad idea," Marion answered. "That way we can at least leave you alone, and if you snap at us we understand that it's nothing personal."

Eve sniffed. "That's stupid—nobody's going to do that."

"No, it isn't likely," I replied. "So what it comes down to is that any kind of human interaction requires a minimum level of courtesy. If you are feeling angry and a stranger asks you a question you don't bark at him. You try to hold down your feelings and give him a civil answer. Don't family members and friends deserve at least that much courtesy?"

"No," Lisa said. "Not if the family member is the reason you're angry."

"Ah, if you're having a fight with somebody that's different," I said. "Were any of you having a fight with me this morning?" I waited for an answer. "It's true that many parents and children have a perpetual battle going on beneath the surface, so it's very hard to get up a little courtesy. We've tried not to let that happen in our family. Do you feel that's going on with us?"

Well, you don't get answers to questions posed like that. *Of course* there is a running struggle between parents and children over the very fulfillment of their roles, but is this so severe that it prevents us from dealing with each other in a courteous way? I didn't think so, and I didn't think my kids did either. I was smugly buttering an English muffin when Lisa let me have it.

"Talk about poisoning the atmosphere," she said. "You aren't always so smiley yourself, you know."

"Yeah, Dad, how about last night?" Eric said.

"You made us wait for dinner while you had a second drink, then you didn't say a word," Eve put in.

"How about it, Dad?" Marion added. "Were you having a fight with us?"

I turned to my wife, who sometimes thinks I overdo the lecture bit. "You, too?" I protested. I had to struggle even to remember the previous night—had I acted so badly? I tried to think about work the previous day—had anything special happened? What had I been so depressed about? No, it wasn't any particular difficulty in my life, perhaps just an accumulation of feelings. "Was I really that unpleasant last night?" I asked.

"Yes," Marion answered.

For a moment I wanted to flare up and say, dammit, I do have some problems that you don't have to cope with, namely some fifty people that work for me, a large part of whom have needs that they don't hesitate to lay on me. But then I thought, no, everything is in proportion. I am an adult and my problems are simply different; they aren't more serious to me than my kids' problems are to them, or my wife's to her. If there was any way Marion or my children could have helped me the night before, they would have. Expressing my need would have produced a little sympathy that might have done the trick.

I had no right to turn off, to freeze them out while I angrily nursed my wounds of the day. It was a struggle for me to acknowledge I was in fact committing an act of aggression. Good God, I thought, who ever said I had to be the jolly daddy all the time? Who can even be cheerful every night of the week? But no, clearly it was more than that. My actions projected more than a normal and acceptable swing in mood: I was, in effect, trying to make somebody "pay" for the resentment that I had built up during the day. I had, indeed, "poisoned" the atmosphere—the very thing I'd just been talking about.

So I told them I was sorry. I can't say that it never happened again. But it was something to work on—and I'm still working on it. Once again the Adult at Eighteen premise was stirring change in me too. If I was determined to teach my kids to live with other people in a more civilized way, then I had to try to set a better example, and I didn't have the rest of my life to do it.

After an initial moment of annoyance I am always glad about these challenges. All of us aspire to become better human beings, and sometimes we have to earn the right to teach our kids. Fear that our children will someday utter the word "hypocrite" is a strong incentive to stop postponing the changes in our own lives that we know we ought to make.

16 ✷

Happy Feelings and
Troubled Friendships

One warm spring afternoon I picked up my son at high school to go
to a ball game, but as we drove off he seemed preoccupied. "Everything go all right today?" I asked.

"I guess so," he said.

"Lots of schoolwork hanging over your head?"

"Not especially."

We rode on in silence. "Maybe you've got some other problems.
Most people do."

He thought about it. "Not really."

"Then I guess you must be pretty happy," I said.

He looked up at me for the first time, with a quizzical smile.
"Why do you say that?"

"Well, the absence of pain is the beginning of happiness. If you
don't have any special worries today you may be able to notice that
there are no clouds in the sky, the dogwood if flowering, and we're
on the way to do something that pleases us."

"Is that happiness?"

Now it was my turn to think. "Well, like most emotions, there
isn't any *absolute* quality to happiness. It registers by degrees, something like a thermometer. Today I'd say that we have a pretty comfortable reading."

Often it seems that a teenager's world is so filled with frustration, uncertainty, and even fear that we ought to show him how to be aware of those days when his worries and angers have moderated. He can't always be holding his breath, braced for a blow of fate. We all need to relax our guard, reasonably confident that for today at least the world is not going to oppress us.

How do we teach this? We can rejoice out loud more often. "I had a terrific day at work. Got a lot of old problems resolved. On a scale of ten I'd say it was about a seven." We use that Scale of Ten at our house; it seems a bit foolish in a way, and yet it gives us some rough yardstick with which to measure ourselves and our feelings. Often enough someone in the family will rejoin: "Well, I had an absolutely *lousy* day. Mine was about a . . . *four*." The complainer always seems to pause to add it up; interestingly enough, I can't remember anybody ever putting a "bad day" as low as two. If you have to stop to count, you generally find some positives, and anyway most people, especially kids, are absolutely sure that someday they're going to have a *disaster*—and they want to save those low numbers on the scale to make sure they get plenty of sympathy when it happens.

No matter how we communicate, if parents can somehow convey that even an average day ranks better than 50 percent in "good news," then we tell our kids that life should have an optimistic cast to it. We say we are sorry when things go wrong, but tomorrow everything is likely to snap back to normal again, and normal is not so bad.

Of course our kids have to understand that there's more to happiness than the absence of pain and more to it than simple contentment. Life is also filled with epiphanies of *joy*, and we have to learn how to connect them up so they form a larger surge of feeling which lasts for hours, or perhaps even days. How do we teach *this?* About all we can do is hope that we experience some of our own profound moments of joy in front of our children. They see and remember more than we think.

One of the clearest memories I have of my father is a "close-up" of his face filled with wonder and exultation. It was during the lean days of the Depression when I was about eight, and dad had got me up before dawn to go duck hunting with him. He was sharing his job in the gas station at the time with two other men and thus, although he wasn't a great hunter, had borrowed a shotgun to shoot "a little something for the table."

We hadn't settled ourselves into the reeds at the edge of a lake in the dawn half-light when a wave of thirty giant geese swept over us in a perfect V at an unusually low altitude, filling the air with haunting, unforgettable honking. I had never seen such majestic, purposeful birds—Canadian snow geese rarely visited our part of the country. I was fascinated, of course, but I didn't really know how impressed I should be until I heard a little moan of awe from my father and looked up to find him transfixed, as the flock circled to gain height and then moved rather slowly across the sky into silhouette against the sunrise.

"Ain't that *somethin'?*" my father said, the shotgun still at his feet. "*Ain't that somethin'?*" Driving back that morning, I could see that it was not important to my father that we were going home empty-handed. He was still filled with the grandeur of that moment at dawn.

What did this incident do for me, exactly? I doubt if the flight of snow geese in itself inspired me in the way it did my father— possibly he brought some earlier emotion to this experience. But surely I learned something from his face that morning—the realization that it's not only permissible but desirable to feel and express pure joy, wherever we may find it; and we can find it in many ways.

An important key to happiness, it seems to me, lies in the feeling that (a) the world knows we are alive, (b) that it accepts us, and (c) at least a part of the world also likes and even loves us. In the beginning it is chiefly the parents who perform all of these functions for the child: we are his "world." But very quickly our children grow past this stage, and in the teen years it is often one or two or three good friends, of both sexes, who help our children to define themselves as individuals and enable them to generally "feel good."

In the periods when these relationships are going well, our children are likely to look like good candidates for early adulthood. But then some crisis arises in the friendship and a confident teenager suddenly appears lost, helpless, and much too miserable ever to manage life independently.

What can we do?

Not a lot directly. You may recall how tough it was to patch up a quarrel back when they were five years old. Now it's impossible. All we can do is make an extra gesture of love and support to give them the subconscious message that even if they have slipped back to "stage one" for the moment, this emotional base is as secure as ever. If we try to interfere directly, even to give advice, or to "steer" the relationship, we are eroding the learning experience.

Were Marion and I smart enough to avoid this emotional trap? No, of course not. If a child considers you a friend and feels distressed and wants to talk about something, you have to listen. Often we feel grateful that the teen is willing to reveal himself at all, even though we realize that the feelings could better be shared with one of his peers. Slowly, however, my wife and I have been learning to be responsive but passive listeners, and when all the unhappy details have been recited we try not to offer a solution, even if the teen insists he wants an answer.

Teenage kids can't accept many of our solutions in any case, no matter how inspired they might be. We've all *tried*, only to experience the exquisite frustration of a hundred "yes, but" reasons why our ideas can't work. Inadvertently we've bumped up against the separation process again. Even though they invited us into the problem, our teens suddenly realize that they can't accept any more "orders" from us no matter how tactfully we phrase our suggestions.

Does this mean that we can't talk to them about the nature of friendship? No, we should give them whatever principles and insights we have, especially when friendship deals with a male-female relationship. We can do this best, I think, by listening carefully and then finding a casual opening later to talk in a general way about the problem at hand.

For example, when Lisa was eighteen I once overheard her complaining to her mother how "selfish" one of her boy friends was, how the conversation always had to turn to *his* problems, and how whenever she placed the slightest demand upon him a storm blew up. I was only passing through the room at the time and thus didn't hear what Marion had to say, if anything; but a week later I had a chance to talk about the nature of friendship. I was typing a letter when Lisa walked into the room. She asked what I was doing, and I replied that I was writing to a friend I'd known for more than thirty years.

"Wow," she said.

"Does thirty years sound like a long time to have a friendship?" I asked.

She considered. "No, probably not, if both friends are the same sex."

"I don't think the fundamentals of friendship have that much to do with sex."

"You're kidding," she said.

"No," I answered. "The biggest problem is for two people to agree on who's the Giver and who's the Taker. It's a kind of unconscious decision that two people make as to what they want out of the relationship."

"Why does there have to be one person who does all the giving?" Lisa asked. "Why can't people do *both*?" Lisa had brought the problem down to relate directly to her needs, although ostensibly we were still speaking generally. My effort now was to keep the discussion apparently on a general level so that she would not feel I was prescribing for her.

"Well, ideally both friends would give equal amounts of their time, energy, sympathy, and love, or whatever," I said. "But life is rarely in equilibrium, even when you get to be my age. Most people mean well—it's just that their *perceptions* are slightly askew. Most of us believe we are giving 50 percent to our friends and loved ones, when in fact we may only be giving 30 percent. Equally, many of us think we are asking only what's fair from our friends, when actually we may be demanding 70 percent of the relationship."

"I don't like putting percentages on a friendship," Lisa protested.

"No, I agree," I said. "I was just trying to show why no relationship can be perfectly fair. The Givers in a relationship, of course, are generally aware of the situation, but the Takers aren't."

"Yeah," she said thoughtfully.

"Now, this doesn't mean that you can't still have a friendship. Maybe the situation is only temporary, for example. Suppose your friend is basically a generous person but right now he seems overwhelmed with terrible problems. Everything seems to be going so badly that he doesn't stop to analyze where his love and support is coming from. He simply breathes a resentful grunt of relief that "it's about time" life gave him some good news. This situation is not fair to the Giver, of course, but think of it as a situation in which a lifeboat has capsized. If your friend has to struggle to keep his head above water, then it's understandable that he doesn't have much time to look around to see who else might need a life preserver."

"How long does this have to go on?"

"I don't know. How big a person are you? Most people don't have to swim for their lives forever; eventually their feet touch bottom. Maybe then your friend can afford to look around him and see who helped him when he needed it."

"I'm beginning to wonder if there aren't just two kinds of people in the world—swimmers and non-swimmers," my daughter answered gloomily.

"No, that's too cynical. If you're going to set up categories, I think it would be better to say that there are two kinds of friendship: All Seasons and Special Purpose. For example, I have Business Friends and Tennis Friends and Next-Door-Neighbor Friends and even Old Drinking Buddy Friends. In each of these cases we can be very warm and even close, but it is understood by both sides that our relationship is limited to a specific time or place or function. These kinds of friendships operate well because we don't try to load too much on them. As you get older you get more skilled indentifying from the start whether the friendship has to be limited or whether it can flower into something marvelous which involves every aspect of our personality. The Friends for All Seasons are the ones that can last thirty years."

"This letter you're writing—are you a Giver or Taker with him?" she asked.

"Right now I'm a Giver, because I'm writing him a letter. He doesn't write letters—he phones—and it seems to me that I say more in my letters than we can in a quick long-distance phone call. But that doesn't matter, because over a period of time the relationship swings back and forth. I can remember some occasions when I was a 90 percent Taker, and he gave gladly."

Lisa smiled. "That's really nice."

I waited.

Finally it came out. "What if you aren't sure that the other party ever will be capable of giving enough?"

"Then you have to consider whether you made a mistake in your categories," I said. "Maybe he or she was a Special Purpose Friend from the start. The person had a certain charm which appealed to you, but now he isn't charming any more. Life is full of mistakes like this, and as long as we give more than we get we never have to feel guilty about simply chalking this relationship up to experience."

"That may be all right for a friend-friend," she said. "It's not so easy if it's a boy friend."

"The more emotion we put into a relationship the harder it is to admit that we may have made a mistake. But the same two categories still apply."

"I wonder," Lisa said.

"You know, it's perfectly possible that we unconsciously select friends we know will require us to be the Giver. We deliberately seek out this role."

"Why would anybody do that?"

"It's more blessed to give than to receive, right? To be an angel of mercy? All this 'giving' also means that we have the right to do a lot of advising, and this too has its psychic rewards. It's a kind of power."

"Are you talking about me? Is this what I've been doing?" she asked.

"I don't know much about your various boy friends. I've liked them well enough, but how do I know how things really work between you? It would be presumptuous for me to say, anyway. But if you can see a pattern in which you end up mothering your boy friends, then maybe that's something for you to think about."

"It's not *mothering*, exactly."

"No, but maybe it's not a relationship of psychological equals either. You may be shying away from boys who offer too much of a challenge."

"Maybe I don't need any more challenge in my life right now."

"Perhaps not. But then you can't feel unhappy about the essentially one-way relationships that you have. When you're ready for something a little richer you'll know what to look for."

"How will I know him?"

I had to laugh. "Honey, I don't have the faintest idea. I've just been talking in generalities. What I've said may not apply to you at all. On the other hand, you might try a boy friend who's a completely different type, just to see what happens."

"Uh-huh," my daughter said. She looked at me curiously as if to wonder how this conversation had got started anyway, and then we went down to dinner.

Did she try a different type of boy friend? Yes. As she moved through the college years, we met quite a varied selection. Did this one conversation influence her decisions? I doubt it, and yet the total effect of what Marion and I had to say through the years about the nature of relationships certainly did. As I look back, it seems to me that my daughter has done very well in educating herself about the various kinds of giving and loving in a close relationship. I'm sure now that when she finally gets married it will be to a man who is also her Friend for All Seasons.

17 ❊

Listen, Child, to the Wonder
of Your Ancestors

Ours is not a tradition-directed society. Our fathers and forefathers hardly matter; we care only who *we* are—and what we can do. This is the glorious promise of America; and also the crushing burden it lays upon its children. We are all required to invent ourselves.

Unhappily, our children have even fewer building blocks to work with than we did. Unlimited geographic mobility, for example, may be an economic blessing but it is hurtful psychologically. Our children may have lived in a half dozen houses or apartments in various parts of the country, and they may never have seen the old family homestead we grew up in. They have no sense of *place*—no piece of ground in which the family tree has sent down its roots.

The nuclear family of today offers children only mother and father as role models. Grandparents, uncles and aunts, and cousins make only occasional visits—if they come at all. The family tree thus seems a mere sapling; there is not much to cling to or shelter under. And yet since parents feel a connecting link with others before us who bore our name and blood, we have an obligation to our sons and daughters to communicate this feeling before they have to ask: "Who am I?" If the immediate family is part of the bedrock of their security in these troubled, changing times, our kids need to understand that

Family consists of more than two generations. It is not only relief but pleasure to understand that Family is a living entity which endures.

It's fashionable now to go searching for your "roots." If you are black I can see how important it might be to trace your connection back to a free people in Africa; but to most white children in middle-class America it may be more useful to understand the recent family continuity, to know that your parents' parents were real people, and their parents before them. (Genealogy beyond this point becomes a study of history; it can be a fascinating hobby, but probably not for teenagers.)

Marion's mother is still alive, and for some years when she came to dinner I encouraged her to talk about her mother and father and her grandparents and what she remembered before our century was born. But people in their eighties ramble, forget, and repeat themselves, and it wasn't long before our kids were rolling their eyes in boredom. We made them listen as long as we could, but it soon became evident that living history was something more than they deserved.

Perhaps at this late day there was no way Grandmother K. could communicate the essence of her life and times to our children. But at least they would remember her as a person. Of my parents, however, they knew little or nothing. And so one Sunday I got a box of snapshots out of the attic. I decided I'd pick out a hundred pictures for an Ancestor Album and try to tell a story with them—to make my parents and grandparents real in some way. A small, neat package of recent ancestors—not much, but better than nothing.

It was hard to make a selection—most old Kodak snapshots show people gawking stiffly into the camera from too far away. But as I sorted, I began to see some hope. For example, here I am sitting on a tricycle, at about age five. The loving way my father has his arm across my shoulder tells it all. Here's a 1939 shot of him I took as a teen with my old Brownie as he posed proudly in front of his new Mobil gas station, and another candid shot as he reaches intently under a customer's hood. "He really gave service—worked 12–14 hours a day," I wrote with a felt pen across the top and bottom of the photo.

I began to add comments on some of the photos of my mother. Here she is as a young girl. *A beauty at age fifteen*, I wrote. Then as a new mother holding me proudly for the camera: *How she loved that baby!* On another photo of the two of us in Kalamazoo, circa 1936, I said, *Lived together in 1 rm while she finished college.* Here she is in cap and gown: *Happy as she got B.A. degree at age forty!* In a snapshot of Mother touching an Alaskan totem pole I wrote, *Energy and curiosity never flagged;* as she questioned a guard at the Tower of London, *Sent her to Europe, 1959;* as she strolled fully dressed but barefoot along a beach, now an old lady, *It wasn't real water unless she waded in it.*

Occasionally, to keep the chronology straight and to further explain, I wrote longer captions on file cards such as: "Dad and Mom met at a boarding house and were married a week later. He was a young widower of twenty-two whose wife had died after only a few months of marriage. A sixth-grade dropout, he was impressed with Mom's two years of college and culture; she by his devilish blue eyes and the chance to 'make something out of him.' Never were two people so mismatched—for ten years. After the divorce she focused her energies (titanic) on making something out of her son. When he fled for his life, she returned to teaching, incredibly successful in breaking through to hundreds of kids in the poorest rural areas of Michigan, Colorado, and New Mexico. Nature study, poetry, music were subjects she loved most, but she preached gutsy self-improvement in all forms to kids & adults equally."

My father did remarry eventually, and I've included a photo of him gazing quizzically at my stepmother. To explain that look, I wrote: "He sighed once that although he'd always loved women he never had much luck marrying them." The Album, which began with what few photos I have of my grandparents, then goes on with snapshots which detail my own growing up and later world travel as a young man. The whole takes no more than fifteen minutes to thumb through and read; when you are finished you have a sense of Wilbur and Alice as people—each powerful but, in his own way, limited. (You also know something more about the man who wrote the captions.)

My kids get out the Ancestor Album every year or two, usually to show some friend, and then complain that there isn't more of it. Marion swears she's going to assemble one for her side of the family. If you have a pile of miscellaneous photos, organize them— unselected they have no interest for kids, and without captions they have no meaning. Of course a photo story can hardly do justice to all that my parents were. (Yes, I would like to write about each of them at length, but it's still too soon. At what age, I wonder, can we finally see our parents fully and dispassionately?)

To make the generations come alive we have to cross-examine our oldest surviving relatives as to what they recall or have heard about the earliest members of the family. Very little is written down, even in family Bibles, and if you don't hear it now, and repeat it, this information may be lost forever to our children and their offspring.

Here is the true story of three generations of women in my mother's family, as I finally pieced it together. I started to write it in a letter to Eve once when she was away but didn't finish until a few months later. One night after dinner I read it aloud to Eve, Lisa, and Marion:

"Dear daughter, you come from a line of very strong women. Have I ever mentioned that your great-great-grandmother, Hannah McCumber, walked from New York to Michigan when she was ten years old? Does this interest you? If, like so many other young people, you are trying to decide who and what you are, you need to look back as well as around. No generation is an island, and there may be more of Hannah in you and me than we think, a strength that we don't know we have."

"She was only *ten?*" Eve broke in, astonished.

"Yes, but of course she didn't make the journey alone. The story begins in 1840. Although the Erie Canal had been open for some years, our family was too poor to hire a flatboat. And so, intent on a fresh start 'out west' with unlimited free land, they piled everything on a covered wagon, the original Conestoga made in Conestoga, Pennsylvania. It was pulled by two old and very tired oxen, moving very slowly—maybe only a mile or two an hour. Because the wagon was so overloaded with furniture everyone had to walk except Hannah's mother, who was seven months pregnant when they left.

"It took them three months to make a trip we can drive in a single day now if we want to. Hannah's sister was born somewhere in Ohio, and the family finally settled in a little clearing near Niles, Michigan, then nothing more than a wilderness trading post. All through her teens, because there were no boys in the family, Hannah helped her father clear the virgin forest, snaking logs behind an ox, burning stumps, and then taking her turn behind a wooden plow at the first furrow of the unbroken land.

"When it came time for Hannah to marry, the man she picked was a one-legged fiddler named Walker—"

"Couldn't she do any better than *that?*" Lisa demanded.

"Was Hannah pretty?" Eve asked.

"I don't know," I replied. "The only photos we have were taken when she was an old, old lady. Anyway, as I get the story, Walker was a charming guy. By trade he was a cobbler, reputed to make the softest shoes in the whole state of Michigan. But apparently what he really liked to do was fiddle at dances and weddings and hop around on his peg with the ladies. Anyway, Hannah inherited the farm from her father and outlived her husband by a good many years. According to one letter I read dated 1921, just before her death, she still milked her cow twice a day and 'kept a lively twinkle in her eye,' so I guess she wasn't too dissatisfied with her life.

"She had one son named Charles, born in 1867," I went on. "He was my grandfather, and I first remember him about 1934 when he was already in his late sixties. He owned his own truck and until he died at eighty-four he peddled loads of grain from Indiana to small mills in Michigan. Every time he drove up in front of our house he'd slam on his brakes in a great cloud of dust and blow the horn until we all came out. He wanted everybody in the neighborhood to know he was there. Since we didn't have a guest room he had to sleep with me, and I never quite got used to the idea that when he undressed for bed he just took off his shoes and pants. He wanted to get on the road in a hurry at 4 A.M., he insisted, so he hopped under the covers with me still wearing his long underwear, his socks, his shirt, and even his tie."

This brought smiles of disbelief from everybody. "I'll tell you more about him later, but I want to get back to the girl he married," I said. "She was a real beauty named Abba White from South Bend, Indiana, and I never got to know her because she died before I was born. Apparently my grandmother was very independent for her time. She never finished high school but six weeks at a 'normal college' was enough to qualify her as a schoolmistress. She had to handle all eight grades at once in a one-room schoolhouse. One minute she'd be quoting poetry to some of the sensitive young girls and the next minute she'd be beating up an overgrown farm boy because he'd 'sassed' her. Abba's father wanted her and Charles to settle down on the family farm with him. You know, that farm today forms part of the campus of Notre Dame University."

"Dad, you wouldn't put us on, would you?" Lisa asked.

"No, it's a fact. The family always used to kid about how 'the Catholics' had taken advantage of us when we were nothing but dumb hardscrabble farmers. The idea was that they'd bought the White farm about the same way the Dutch swindled Manhattan from the Indians. My mother once threatened to write to Notre Dame to see if they wouldn't offer me a scholarship in compensation for the land they'd 'stolen' from us."

"Did they?" Eve asked.

"No, it was a joke—one of the few I can ever remember my mother making. Anyway, Charles, or C. M. as he was known, wasn't going to be any farmer. He took Abba off to Benton Harbor, Michigan, where at age twenty-three he did pretty well as a real-estate speculator. Eventually he got into patent medicine. I have on my desk a four-ounce glass-stoppered bottle which once contained Walker's Relief. It cured 'Congestive Chills, Bowel Difficulties, Sick Headaches, Neuralgia, Rheumatism, Colic, Croup, Bronchitis,

Diphtheria, etc.' and could be taken either externally or internally. It was also widely advertised for Ladies' Complaint. My aunt once confessed that Walker's Relief was 90 percent alcohol and the rest a 'mystery formula' which her father wouldn't divulge to anyone, except that she knew red pepper was involved. At any rate, about the turn of the century the federal Pure Food and Drug Act was passed, and 'Medicine Walker' (as he was known throughout those states) decided to write off his inventory and try another line of business.

"One spring day in 1901, C. M. strolled into the house and told Abba he had just made a down payment on eighty acres of farmland 'up in the logging country' and she should prepare to move. By this time Abba had borne three children. She had a strong character, and while no record of the ensuing argument over C. M.'s unilateral decision survives, we do know she was not happy about returning to the drudgery of a farm, especially in a primitive, just-logged-off piece of sandy scrub a hundred miles to the north, far from civilization. But C. M. told her he was broke, and that settled it.

"She loaded everything in the house into a railroad boxcar— piano, children, and all—and rode *with* them as the train chugged off. It took a week, and how she managed to prepare meals and keep small children safe and quiet in a freight car I don't know. C. M. drove on ahead in a fast buggy to get things ready. The new homestead was three miles from the nearest settlement, a tiny town of four hundred souls (it has that same population today). Here Abba became the complete pioneer woman of a generation earlier. Unlike Hannah, she didn't have to plow the land, but little else was changed. For example, she sewed her sheets, curtains, and the children's dresses out of a single bolt of cloth. She split her kindling wood, pumped water from the well, and heated it on the kitchen stove, then bathed her babies in the washtub in the woodshed. She boiled syrup from her thirty maple trees, and induced her hens to lay eggs in winter by feeding them warm water. The day began with a good table, piled with fried pork, potatoes, eggs fixed three ways, oatmeal porridge, peach jam, and bread baked fresh before breakfast. The local schoolteacher boarded at Abba's house, providing a small cash income and cultural stimulus. Abba was big on self-improvement for everyone in the family, and herself studied home courses on such things as astronomy.

"Not everybody went on to high school in those days, but there were no dropouts in Abba's family. The kids walked three miles *each way*, and in the winter when the drifts got too deep she rented them rooms in town till the storm blew over. She sang, played piano, talked wisely and gently to her children, but was too embarrassed to tell her daughters the simple facts of menstruation. She bore eight children in all, sometimes with only the help of a neighbor woman."

"I never would have made it," Marion sighed.

"Oh, come on, Mom. You would have made a great pioneer," Lisa insisted.

"Eight children and all the rest, maybe," Marion said. "But not baking bread every morning before breakfast."

"How about you, Evie?" I inquired. "Do you think you could have been a pioneer?"

Eve does not really approve of hypothetical questions. "I guess so," she replied finally. "What choice did people have?"

I nodded "My grandmother died at age forty-four of an unknown stomach ailment, which might have been appendicitis—the doctor arrived late and couldn't make up his mind. Medical service was not only crude in rural areas—it was almost nonexistent. Abba's family was left in the hands of my Aunt Olive, her oldest child, then only seventeen . . . How does that grab you? Seven brothers and sisters ranging down to a tiny baby, and C. M. away from home in Chicago most of the time buying and selling grain and fruit. Olive put aside her own ambitions (and a serious beau) as a matter of course—and stepped into her mother's heavy, high-button shoes."

"How did she feel about giving up her own life to take over the family?" Eve asked.

"She wasn't too happy about it, as you might imagine, and apparently she was a hard taskmaster for the younger members of the family," I said. "That's one reason my mother got married in such a hurry."

"People were prisoners of their families," Lisa said.

"Yes, in a way," Marion answered, "but mainly they were prisoners of poverty. And it wasn't all bad, either. Families were big in those days and they gave lifelong support to each of their members. But go on about Olive."

"Well, she eventually married a fine man, not only a college graduate but an ex–county school superintendent. They had no children, and they worked the farm all of their days. In fact, your Great-Aunt Olive lives there now, a widow, aged eighty-seven, still as dedicated to her land and to her family as on the day Abba charged her with the responsibility.

"She's been totally blind for five years. My Aunt Leona and Uncle Vern drive up from Muskegon thirty miles away twice a week to bring her food. Olive warms up the frozen dishes on her electric stove, injects herself daily with insulin, and absolutely refuses to go to any kind of nursing home. She listens to television, but not those silly situation comedies. She likes the news, the talk shows, and the serious interview programs like 'Meet the Press.'

"Can you put yourself in her place, kids? Most of us are desolate if we have to spend half a day entirely by ourselves—with our eyes open. But this charged-up old lady doesn't know the meaning of self-pity. Occasionally her neighbor, who farms Olive's land on shares, will drop in to discuss the price of corn or what should be done about the nest of pheasants in the corner of the hay field, but last time I visited Olive no one came to the door and the phone did not ring for three days. And yet she was content. When I asked her how she managed it she seemed surprised. 'I don't know,' she said. 'I have my books and my TV. I can hear the birds singing and feel the sun on my face. And now you've come to visit me.' "

We talked quite a bit about these earlier generations that night, and they became living people for Lisa and Eve. Sad to say, Olive died a few months later, before I could take my family out to meet her—we always wait too long. But the message of these three great women was clear to my daughters. As I wrote in my letter to Eve, "The same blood and spirit surges in you. Your problems are different, surely, and at times they will seem more psychic than physical. But when your life becomes frantic and you are full of worry and depression, think back to the women who came before you. They met the challenge, and they prevailed and so will you."

18 ☀

Stories About Leaving Home

If we really expect our children to leave home emotionally as well as physically, some of our conversations should deal explicitly with this subject. When our kids were young they liked to hear about the year Mommy spent in a girls' boarding school when she was just about their age, and how she handled the feeling of homesickness. I talked about my summers at the YMCA camp—how I almost drowned swimming across the lake for my canoe test, and the terror I felt when one afternoon, as I was lying in my bunk, some kids put a blue racer down my back and I had to lie rigid for five minutes while it crawled out my pants leg. As they moved through high school Marion recounted her adventures as an apprentice in a commercial art studio, surviving alone in a big city like Chicago, and then told about life on a bicycle as she pedaled across Europe, and how she and a girl friend later had visited oases in Algeria deep in the Sahara, where few tourists had ventured.

Our kids loved the idea that, yes, it's kind of scary out there but also marvelously free and exciting. And no matter what the problems, there is always a way to handle them. My son, like most men, lusts for the adventure of travel, and so the first spreading of my own wings at age sixteen had a special appeal for him. "Tell about going to California and riding the rods and being hungry," he would say, and he never seemed to mind my shameless moralizing. This is the way the story went the first time:

The Glory of the Mashed Potatoes

"Every young person should be hungry at least once. I don't mean hungry because you are dieting; I mean hungry because you are alone in a strange city, don't have any money, and haven't eaten in thirty-six hours. Suddenly life gets very *real*. Money has been nothing but handy little pieces of paper before. Now, all at once, you can't believe that everybody you pass on the streets has his pockets full of cash, and you don't have any, and they can go into stores and buy anything they want, absurd things they don't even need, *and you don't have anything to eat!* How can life be structured in this way? How can it be so unfair?

"The trip started in late June a week after I'd graduated from high school. I had a buddy who had moved to California and was unhappy; I decided I'd hitchhike out there from Michigan, see a little of the Hollywood lotus land, then talk Harry into coming back with me, and we'd join the Marines together. It was an incredible journey—not as easy as it might be today because World War II had brought on tire rationing that year, and people weren't taking any long trips in their cars. (Gas rationing was to come soon.)

"Trucks were the hitchhiker's best bet, and in fact on my first day out a crazy young Texan let me drive his big ten-wheel 'semi' while he took a nap. Did I know how to handle a rig? Sure, I said, and a minute after we'd exchanged places he was snoring hard, exhausted from driving all night. Steering a truck is not a problem, but no matter how hard I sweated I couldn't double-clutch fast enough to get that monster into the lowest range of its eight gears. So, overloaded with machine tools for an airplane plant, we'd inch up over hills at about five miles an hour; then we'd come rocketing down like Casey Jones and the runaway locomotive, with me standing on the regular brakes until they smoked. I should have been using the air brakes, but I knew how powerful they were and I was afraid that if I hit them with the wrong touch we might jackknife or roll over. I must have wheeled that thing fifty miles like that, wringing wet with sweat and my arms aching, but excited! I loved it—the ultimate in teenage machismo. I didn't even dare blow the horn for fear that I'd wake up the Texan and he'd make me go back to being just a kid passenger.

"Then as I came thundering down a long hill about 70 mph toward a small town, a farmer on a tractor pulled out ahead of me. I could see we were both going to hit the bottom of the hill and a narrow bridge about the same time. With one eye on the Texan beside me I blasted the horn for the first time. My trucker didn't even budge—but neither did the farmer. Wow! I was hopping up and down on that seat, racked with indecision, as we hammered down on that little scrunched-up figure in overalls stubbornly chugging along on his tractor. Obviously I had to hit the air brakes. I stroked that lever like I was petting a newborn kitten and—what do you know!—it did stop us, and we didn't jackknife. Just about hurled my sleeping host through the windshield, though. But he was a nice guy and took it pretty well (even bought me supper that night). The farmer didn't take it so well; the noise of those tires screaming to a halt and leaving about an inch of rubber on the road scared him so badly that he lurched into a ditch. As we drove past he was having hysterics, shaking his fist at the Texan as he climbed over me in the cab to take the wheel."

Eric was grinning in appreciation at this point; I paused and tried to be serious: "You know, son, all this sounds slightly funny now, but in fact I could have killed that farmer and the Texan too, and myself. Just one slight stroke of the hand on that air brake or a turn of the steering wheel. That's what parents are always worrying about—that kids get excited by the power of the machine they're driving and don't realize what a narrow margin of control they have—even with the family car and at fairly modest speeds."

"We get all that in driver's education in school, dad," Eric protested. Maybe so, but I resolved that the next time we were out driving together I'd try to demonstrate dramatically just how difficult it is to stop when something unexpected pops up in front of you. "Tell about the Indians," Eric prompted gently. (Apparently I'd told at least part of this story earlier—parents lose authority when they can't remember.)

"I had another, safer adventure a couple of days later," I went on. "My ride dropped me in the middle of an Arizona desert. It was noon with the temperature at 105 degrees—no shade and no signs of life. Hours passed without any cars, I could see great mirage sheets of water cascading across the highway in the distance, and the buzzards overhead began to circle lower. Finally an old rusty farm truck limped into sight, and I stood in the middle of the road waving my suitcase and wouldn't let them drive past.

"Turned out to be a bunch of Navajo Indians moving somebody's household goods to another reservation. They hardly spoke any English but signaled that it was OK for me to toss my suitcase in the back and climb aboard. But when we pulled into a small town I had to return the favor. Liquor stores in that part of the world followed an old frontier custom of not selling booze to Indians (maybe that's changed now, I don't know). My new friends gave me some money and wanted me to buy them a bottle of whiskey, but I figured that if this was all the ride I had heading west, maybe wine would be a smarter choice. The liquor-store owner looked at me funny, then at the Indians in the truck out in front, then at my fake Michigan identification which said I was twenty-two years old, but he sold me a gallon of the cheapest red port wine he had.

"I tell you five braves and I got bombed in the sun as we roared across the desert in the back of that truck. The truck was a jumble of beat-up kitchen and bedroom furniture, boxes, clothes, and bags of grain. An old boy passed out on some bedsprings while they were teaching me what I took to be war chants; and then, I swear to you, one young brave actually got up on top of the dresser and did a rain dance or something in his cowboy boots. Anyway, it was a pretty neat dance with a lot of fast footwork in front of the dresser mirror; I was going to get up there and take a turn, but just then we began to ease into Flagstaff and I figured we ought not to attract any more attention than necessary. They invited me out to the reservation, and I probably should have said yes.

"After a dozen more rides which weren't nearly as much fun I got to Los Angeles and there, in a decaying section of town, in a run-down YMCA, experienced the exquisite horror of a night with bedbugs. It's not that the bugs actually hurt when they bite, it's just that you imagine they are *creeping* all over you, all the time. I kept leaping out of bed every ten minutes cursing and jerking on the light to catch them. But a bedbug is fast and you almost never see him. After a while you think you are going mad, and that maybe it's all in your mind, except there are those tiny little spots of blood on the sheet. Your blood.

"Anyway, about 3:45 A.M. I gave up trying to sleep and went out. The cops picked me up then for standing around looking suspicious outside a sleazy strip-tease joint. I really wanted to go in but was afraid I'd have to buy a drink at two dollars a shot or something. Just like you see on TV now, the cops had my hands up against a wall while they frisked me, and they kept yelling questions at me about what I'd been doing there at that hour, pressing my nose up against the front window like a kid looking into a candy store. They didn't believe me about the bedbugs.

"At first I thought they must be looking for a suspect about my age or something, but when they wouldn't listen to anything I had to say I began to see that I wasn't a *person* to them at all—I was just a body walking around at a suspicious time and place. I hadn't done anything but I was presumed guilty rather than innocent. I felt helpless and diminished—and then angry because they made me feel that way. People in the ghetto must feel this way about the police quite often."

"That's why they call them pigs," my son said.

"Maybe. But, on the other hand, when you stop to think about the problems of being a cop in a big city you realize it's the toughest job in the world. So it's not fair to dehumanize the cops by calling them pigs, is it? They're individuals too—under great stress. It's another one of those situations where we can't make easy judgments even when we get pushed around ourselves. Anyway, after a number of other educational incidents I finally got to the Napa Valley in northern California and found old Harry raring to go. We pooled our money and figured we could make it home to Michigan, but we were wrong. In Wyoming all the long-range traffic petered out because of the rationing, and after we'd stood a day and a half in one spot, through rain and dark and sunrise, we got the idea there just wasn't going to *be* any more hitchhiking. So the two of us calmly walked into the center of the railroad yards and in full daylight climbed on a freight train. I think the superintendent up in the tower must have been so astonished at our naïveté that he didn't bother to send a railroad dick to throw us off. When I told my father about it later, *he* was astounded: When he'd tried it once back in the twenties not only had he got clubbed on the head but he'd been pushed off the train at 20 mph as it rounded a curve. Maybe they saw the school pennant on my suitcase, or maybe no bum—with or without suitcase—would ever be dumb enough to climb in an open gondola car to ride across the western plains.

"We couldn't find any of those nice comfortable boxcars that the *Grapes of Wrath* families in the movie had ridden in. Everything was sealed. The only thing left was an empty open car which had been used to haul chemical fertilizer. It was about forty feet long and had steel sides twelve feet high, so you couldn't see any scenery without climbing up and hanging on desperately for a few minutes. You lay in the bottom staring up at the clouds, hour after hour, feeling as if you were in a giant casket and getting closer and closer to your Maker.

"For five hours the train didn't move, and when it did we rode all night, miserably cold, constantly thrown about as the train stopped, jerked, and switched. And dirty! At 8 A.M. the next morning we were so dirty from the engine's soot that we were afraid we'd never get a ride in an automobile again. We clambored out wearily and found some breakfast at a diner, figuring that we must be half-way to Chicago by now. We discovered that after seventeen hours in that open-air tomb we had moved just one hundred miles. My respect for the railroads has never recovered.

"So, you can imagine the kind of state we were in by the time we finally shuffled into Chicago. It had been fearsome hard going, and had taken a long time. We had eaten cheaper and cheaper as we moved east, and then less and less. As we walked about the Loop now we realized that it had been thirty-six hours since our last food, and we had only seventeen cents to buy a meal for both of us. I counted the money again; finally, for fear we'd lose it, I tied it in the corner of my handkerchief like mothers used to do for little kids. One side of my stomach seemed to be gnawing on the other; it actually hurt, and I imagined my belly was starting to distend the way it does in those photos of starving children in India and Africa. I felt light-headed and my knees seemed to wobble.

"Of course most of this was just in my mind; shipwreck victims survive three weeks and more without food as long as they have water. But for the first time I really was coming to grips with fundamentals. All the complaints and problems I'd had faded away to nothing. I was discovering a great empathy for people who were poor but I also acquired sudden respect for those who weren't. Money, all at once, was not something casual, or as some kids see it now, contemptible. It was food. Here I was just 150 miles from home and I was *starving* and I didn't care about anything else.

"Why didn't you send home for some money?" Eric asked.

"Because I was too proud. Everybody in my family had advised me not to make this trip."

"But they would have sent it to you if you phoned them," Eric persisted.

"Of course. But I was trying to prove something to myself." Eric made no comment, so after a moment I went on: "Neither Harry nor I had any doubt that the time had come to spend the seventeen cents. So we staggered down to Skid Row and found what must have been the cheapest cafeteria in Chicago. Going in, we had a big argument. Harry wanted to buy something sweet and spend about an hour eating it, so as to get the most pleasure and energy. I said we simply needed to fill up our stomachs with whatever we could get the most of; and since ten of the seventeen cents was mine, I won.

"Because it was the middle of the afternoon we had the full attention of one grizzled old counterman as we pushed down the cafeteria line, asking the price of every item. I was going to settle for a giant bowl of spinach, but Harry said he couldn't eat spinach. Then our eyes lighted on the mashed potatoes. Ah, we told the man behind the counter, we'll take seventeen cents' worth of mashed potatoes and gravy.

"He'd been getting a little annoyed at our 'picky' pricing, and eyed us now, one empty tray between us. 'Seventeen cents' worth of mashed potatoes?' he asked.

" 'With gravy,' Harry said. 'Lots of gravy.'

" 'Yeaah, *lots* of gravy,' I breathed.

"Suddenly the counterman got it, and his suspicious frown slid into a smile of serene confidence. His ice cream scoop overflowed with potatoes, and then he made an extra-deep dent in them with a ladle and filled it with gravy. He looked at it a second and added some more gravy. As we reached out for the tray he said, 'Hold it!'

"He broke open a loaf of white bread and piled maybe ten slices on our tray. 'Seventeen cents!' he bawled to the cashier at the end of the tray line. As we paid up, she mumbled something under her breath which we didn't get at the time but which we later deciphered as, 'Leave the sugar,' meaning not to steal the sugar dispenser on our table. Talk about Thanksgiving dinners! You have to be *hungry*, kiddo, before you know how *good* lumpy mashed potatoes and anonymous brown gravy can be. We ate, slowly, but greedily, smacking and savoring every bite. To finish up we had mashed potato sandwiches, with the help of a little ketchup. For dessert we each had a glass of sugar water.

"Harry was all for taking the sugar canister from the table, now that the cashier had put the idea in our heads. Who knew, it might take us another twenty-four hours to get home and we might need the energy. But we decided we didn't want to spoil the generous gift of the counterman. After we had sopped up the last bit of gravy with the last bite of bread, we went back and shook his hand, half hoping he might go ape and offer us a dish of rice pudding or something. But he didn't. He just said, 'You kids oughta stay home where you belong.'

"Which is not the moral of the story. In fact, that long, venturesome trip, climaxed by that providential meal, taught me something. When you are young it takes one hell of a whack before you start registering on the outside world. From that time on I don't think I was ever quite so smug in taking for granted the bounty, the comfort, the pleasures of our middle-class society. Or was quite so morally certain that it was all *owed* to me."

I sat back, a little sorry that I'd ended with a kind of preachment. I needn't have worried—our kids take from us what they need. "How many miles was the trip in all?" Eric asked. "You made it—that's the important thing."

I had to smile at myself. "I guess you're right, son," I said.

19 ✳

Why We Hang On to Them

The biggest problem parents have with Adult at Eighteen is that the deadline seems too early. After the article in the *Reader's Digest* appeared, one mother wrote me: "It may be all right for some children who mature quickly. But others in the same family are moving on their own timetable—they just aren't *ready* at eighteen, and it's cruel to cut them off arbitrarily."

This woman ignores the fact that physiologically our children are ready for adulthood at an early age. All through history—right up to our grandparents' time—children were expected to become men and women at thirteen or fourteen, to do a full share of work, assume adult responsibilities, and, before long, start their own families. Emotional maturity followed as a consequence of assuming the adult role, not vice versa as this mother would have it. Yes, clearly each child has a different timetable, but in a large measure it is the parents who consciously or unconsciously formulate it for him. Some children will become more complete Adults at Eighteen, but all of them can reach some kind of minimum competence, if we insist on it and if we start early enough.

Eighteen is not an arbitrary deadline that I thought up. It is a simple fact of life for most middle-class families. A child goes off to college, and he is *alone.* If we have prepared him to live alone, he copes well and is relatively happy and successful. And we feel happy and successful. If not, not.

Part of the problem is that we parents have no idea how radically different today's college experience is from our own. A school administrator of our time would be both shocked and bewildered at the way a college functions now; even the kids see themselves as far different people than we ever did. Until we actually visited the campus of the college Lisa had chosen, Marion and I had only a hazy notion of what she faced. Suddenly it became clear how far we had come in a single generation, and we were eager to tell our daughter how it had been with us.

If we could talk about the change, perhaps *we* could come to terms with it:

DEAR DAUGHTER,
    When your mother went off to college—really not so very long ago—neither she nor the school thought of it as the final step into adulthood. The college simply assumed *custody* of a young woman, and in fact often seemed more concerned with defending her virtue than enlarging her mind. No friendly young men were assigned rooms on her dormitory floor, or *anywhere* in her building, for example. Liberty was assumed to be license, if not absolute concupiscence, and so surely from the day it was built no man ever saw the inside of your mother's room; she lived, in fact, as cloistered as a nun. She was also not free to come and go as she liked. Men students, quartered panting and frustrated in their own dormitory a safe quarter mile away (or in private rooms in the town), had no restrictions on their hours; but women had to sign out and in, and indeed suffered a 10 P.M. curfew. And that meant 10 P.M. sharp!
    A curfew? Does this seem quaint, even ludicrous? Yes, to me, too, but I remember many a last-minute panic as my date and I scurried up that hill with the campus clock chiming the pumpkin hour. A witch-eyed "house mother" always waited at the sign-in desk at the door, tending both her knitting and the

front steps to make sure the good-night kiss remained chaste. Curfew was better on weekends, though; women students could stay out until midnight or, at really liberal colleges, until 1 A.M. It was presumed that at any more mature hour a girl might lose control of her girdle—if not her moral fibre altogether.

This was in the 1940s, mind you—*just one generation ago.* Neither your mother nor I liked these attitudes or conditions but we accepted them as inevitable. This is the way it *was* with females. Males were sent out into the world, exhorted to "Be a man," "Stand on your own two feet," and "Make a name for yourself." Women were let out of the home sanctuary with great reluctance, and college authorities understood that they were moral surrogates for the parents. The assumption was that women, although they might improve themselves with a few arts and graces, were really in a holding pattern until some enterprising young man flew into their orbit to take over the controls.

Just one generation ago young women were never expected to be functioning adults.

It's hard to grasp this magnitude of change. Today there are no surrogates for parents. Young women who leave home for college or work expect to have sole charge of their emotions, sexual expression, physical safety, mental and spiritual development, and career training. Of course you may feel a little insecure as you leave home for the first time; so does a boy. But your fears are a function of age and inexperience, not of sex. Most young women today have no doubt of their ability to act at least as responsibly as young males in dealing with the world, don't you agree? When, in all the history of mankind, has so great a change taken place within a single generation?

It's all come too fast and too far for us. Most mothers look at their girls—and their sons too—and say to themselves, These kids can't be *that* different. It's all some kind of mass-media swindle, and if we don't keep an arm around them they're going to drown. Many fathers too have locked-in memories of how young people are supposed to conduct themselves. A week after Lisa's college opened a man I know, who also had a freshman daughter, stopped me on the street. He's a top executive in one of the giant foundations which support educational projects, but that wasn't what he had on his mind:

"Boys allowed in your daughter's room at school?" he demanded.

"I assume so."

"Until what hour?"

I had to think about that. "I don't believe there are any restrictions," I answered.

He groaned. "Yeah. Isn't that *unbelievable?* Boys live on the same floor?"

"Yes, with the same bathroom and shower room."

"Jesus, what is this world coming to? It's as if nobody cared. Are they screwing in every room?"

He looked at me with such frustration that I had to be gentle with him. "No, I don't think so."

"How do you know?"

"I don't. But I think Lisa can handle it—she always has."

"She never had unlimited opportunity before," he snapped.

I didn't want to ask questions, to pursue the extent of *his* daughter's entry into adulthood, or his assumption that just because she could be promiscuous she would. So I managed something about Lisa being a fairly responsible human being.

"Lots of luck," he replied. As he walked away, there was a slope of defeat in his back that I'd never seen before.

What a sadness. For him, and for his daughter. Not just because he had no confidence in her ability to handle one of the most elementary problems faced by every young woman, but because clearly neither of them had made a final decision as to when, if ever, she was going to take control of the more complicated and important decisions in her life. The brutal fact is, this man was too late—five years too late. By the time she was eighteen he and his wife should have given their daughter all the assistance any parents can ever give in this area, and they should have been at peace with themselves.

This man also had a son, a year older, whom he had enrolled at Princeton. That Christmas the son came home for vacation, and he never went back. "But why?" my friend asked. "Here I try to give him the best education money can buy, and he doesn't want it! I can't even get him to talk to me about it—he just mumbles that he's got to get his head together. My old man never offered to put me through school—he never gave me a goddamn thing."

It's very *disappointing* for my friend not to be able to pay for his son's education. He wants something of substantial cash value to offer, in part because he feels he's failed to supply his child with much else in the first eighteen years. This isn't true, of course; like most middle-class fathers he not only has supported the family financially but has provided more leadership, strength, and values than he knows. But none of this is apparent to him. As he sees it, a marriage is a partnership in that the wife takes care of the kids and the husband earns the bread. She does most of the day-after-day work of raising the children, and subconsciously she takes most of the credit. The "old man" never gets much of a thank-you from wife or children for all of his sweat.

My friend is typical of many fathers. He doesn't actually cry into his beer, because he knows that even without kids he'd still be getting up to go to work every morning. But he does feel left out. Now, overnight, his star moves into ascendancy. Kids graduate from high school, and the mother's job apparently is done. But a large glob of money is needed; making money is what he's always done best. Father is the only one who can fill *this* family need. His contribution is very visible, and for the first time it may even provoke some gratitude from both child and mother. Suddenly, even though his career may have disappointed him personally, his labors now seem worthwhile. He is *providing*, and everybody recognizes it. It may even be that the larger the tuition the greater his satisfaction; when he complains about the bill to his fellow workers or male friends it is proof of his success that he is able to handle this huge cash drain.

But now, for my friend, everything has gone to hell. Neither daughter nor son has grown up, and there is no telling when they will. They're beyond the point where their parents can talk to them, and the son won't even accept a gift of a college education. How did things fall apart like this?

Part of the problem lies in the father's perception of when and how he is needed. His major function is not to provide money for his children after high school but to offer energy and attention and love in the years just before and during high school. Millions of fathers in this country actually pervert their entire working careers under the illusion that they have to generate a huge treasure for the education of their children. The arithmetic becomes increasingly panicky as each child records another birthday. What's the cost now—is it up to $7,000 a year for the best schools? (Nothing's too good for *my* son and *my* little girl.) Let's see, that makes $28,000 for four years of college—let's not worry about graduate school yet. And since I have three children, that means that I have to save up something like $84,000, only it will probably require more by then because of inflation.

The father doesn't really expect to save up $84,000 for college educations—where can that kind of money come from, after taxes? Nevertheless, he generalizes it into an enormous sum, and thus has an excuse to work twice as hard as before. He has an *obligation*, doesn't he? And therefore he has even less time to spend with his kids as they move into their critical years of development.

Even when his children enter college, when at last they're old enough for him to be able to talk to them and enjoy them, he has to keep his head down and work hard to keep the bucks flowing. He rationalizes it as the supreme sacrifice, but after a while the kids barely notice. They are being taken care of, as they always have been. That's what parents are supposed to do.

If a father in later years should ever point out to his children how his entire work career—his life—was distorted by the need to finance those huge college expenses at that time, the kids would likely answer: "We never told you to distort your life. That was your idea." And they would be right.

20 ✳

Are We Giving Them
Wrong Messages About College?

Ever since they were born we have been telling our children, directly and indirectly, that *of course* they are going to college. It is a middle-class assumption, on which much of our parental teaching is based. Not go to college? Unthinkable. How can our kids possibly survive in this new and frightening world without a college education?

The fact is they may survive very well, and we may be doing them a major disservice by psychologically closing the door to the possibility of *not* going to college—or at least not in the traditional way. If we expect our kids to take control of their lives at age eighteen it's essential that they have an accurate perception of what the world is right now—not the way it was when we were their age.

Maybe Our Kids Shouldn't Go to College at All

We can't bear to think of our children being *poor* for the rest of their lives. At the very least we want them to have the same standard of living that we have. But if we assume that in today's world they have to have a college education to do this, we simply haven't kept up with the facts of life, especially the economic gains of the past ten years. Today millions of non-college men and women are living very well in terms of the things money can buy. If we care to look, they are our neighbors.

For most of our two-hundred-year history America was an agricultural society, and since agriculture has seldom been more than a subsistence (until our time), parents naturally began to put an economic value on an education which could lift their children to the supposed comforts and pleasures of urban life. The trend was continued and even intensified later by the millions of immigrants who, even though they lived miserably in cities, could see hope for their children. In the growing power and complexity of our industrial society, managers and professionals could achieve lifetime earnings double and triple those of their unskilled fathers, and education was the path to these jobs.

Even in the 1960s an average college graduate, despite the expense of his education and four years of lost income, could expect to earn 50 percent more than a high-school graduate during his working life. This is the conventional wisdom of our generation.

But for nearly twenty years now *half* of our high-school graduating classes have been going on to higher education. Right now there are *ten million* kids in college. With only ninety million bodies in the total work force, we have truly reached the point where we have too many chiefs to manage the Indians. Our economy has burgeoned in the postwar years, but the number of college graduates has *exploded*.

And so we come to the simple fact—unheralded in the press—that the economic premium for a college diploma has virtually disappeared. How come nobody has made us aware of this enormous change? A good plumber or TV repairman or even a big-city policeman should produce lifetime earnings equal to or better than the average college graduate. (The census figures of 1970 showed that a majority of men earning $15,000 or more did not have college degrees, and a majority of college grads did not earn $15,000 or more.)

It is hard for us to accept the fact that the old immigrant philosophy of our forefathers has turned sour. "Get education at all costs, and you will rise in the world." Not necessarily. For example, the Department of Labor reports that each year two-thirds of the humanities graduates and three-fourths of the social-science graduates have to take jobs out of their field. What do they do? What first jobs are they finally forced to accept? Low-level computer programmer, bank cashier or clerk, salesman, office-machine operator, truck driver, stenographer, receptionist, waitress, bartender, and so forth.

All this at a time when my local auto dealer is charging $19 an hour for labor to repair my car, when garbage men making $17,000 a year in New York and San Francisco feel they are underpaid, and when a young guy in a T-shirt spends just twelve minutes fixing a pane of glass and a sash cord in my bedroom and slips a bill for $24.50 into my mailbox as he goes out. This month my neighbor's daughter graduated from the Culinary Institute of America at Hyde Park, N.Y., a half mile from FDR's home. It's an attractive school overlooking the Hudson and it demanded just over eighteen months of intensive practice in every kind of cuisine imaginable. The new graduate turned down $15,000 a year to start as assistant chef with a major hotel chain, because she thinks some other offers will be better.

From a strictly financial point of view, you can make a case that the money spent on a college education is a poor investment. Late in the 1960s it cost $17,000, including forgone income, for the average student to earn a degree. Over a forty-year work span this bought a comfortable 11 percent return on the investment after taxes. By 1973 the cost of college had gone up and the economic value of the degree had shrunk so much that a student's investment of his own or his parents' money could be expected to produce only 7.5 percent return, less than the rate available from an investment in prime bonds. And *that* was 1973, before the big surge in higher tuition and inflation.

We also have to consider what the current generation's drastic changes in lifestyle will mean in economic terms. If women are going to pursue a career as a matter of course, have their babies later, produce fewer of them, and go back to work instead of dropping out of the labor force as before, the burden of a middle-class living no longer rests solely on the shoulders of the male. In a two-income family (with lower costs because of fewer children), both partners can afford to work less or take lower-paying jobs, free to seek out a job that really pleases them. A college education may or may not be required..

Obviously, if a young person is attracted by the professions he or she has to have an undergraduate degree to get into medical or law or dental school. And yes, if he plans to be a nuclear physicist, he will have to have graduate training too. And yes, if he wants to climb the corporate executive ladder he had better have the necessary starting credentials. But all of these careers are only a fraction of the total jobs now available which are economically respectable.

It happens in the best of families that some kids just don't want to go on to college—or shouldn't go. Are we too rigid—or too proud—to let these children explore another possiblility with less status? If, in their early teens, they don't have our permission to think in this way, they never will. Oh, come now, you say, am I really trying to encourage my son to become a *plumber?* Even if the plumber who plays in my Friday night poker game is a very civilized fellow indeed (as he is), lives in a bigger house than mine (as he does), and probably nets $40,000 a year? Well, I am a victim of social pressures as much as anyone. The issue never came up with Lisa— she was so hell-bent on college as a springboard to some kind of career that we couldn't have stopped her if we tried. With women's lib in the air, perhaps we never did give her psychological permission not to seek the credentials she might need for a career in the Establishment.

Will it be different with Eric? Probably not. I've tried, in various ways, but Lisa's example and other middle-class pressures may be too strong. In the tenth grade Eric discovered auto mechanics, and he *loved* it. During one parents' night his teacher told how he'd been attempting to encourage boys to take up this trade—and not just the dum-dums, either. Cars are getting so sophisticated that auto dealers can't find competent mechanics at any wage, and if a mechanic can also deal with the public he can almost name his price. The teacher described a two-year "college" for auto service managers in which graduates are regularly snapped up at $25,000 a year. And it doesn't take long to move on to a bigger dealership offering twice this salary plus a share of the profits.

Did all this interest my son? Eric listened politely while I re-counted it, but I'd made a bad mistake. I had told the story at the dinner table. "Ugh!" Eve said. "Are you going to work in a *garage?*"

It will take a strong boy (and stronger parents) to resist pres-sures like these, and so I suppose Eric will go to college when the time comes. Maybe, just maybe, he later will have the courage to realize that education doesn't necessarily preclude work in which your hands get dirty.

We Let Our Kids Believe That a College Degree Has a Market Value

What we mean is that it has negative value, in that young people aren't going to be able to enter the Establishment if they don't have it. But somehow in the process this message gets fuzzed over and turned around, and many kids end up believing that college is truly a four-year apprenticeship to the future good life, that they are learn-ing marketable skills, and when they graduate the real world will be waiting to embrace them. In fact, nobody will—not even the giant corporations.

Several years ago a headline in the *New York Times* caught my eye and I clipped out the article: WHAT DO YALE 'SUPERWOMEN' FIND IN THE JOB MARKET? DISILLUSIONMENT. When Yale went coed for the first time in 1970, only 278 out of 2,850 female applicants were accepted, and so the press dubbed them superwomen. "From the moment I got there," one of them says, "they told me, 'You will succeed, you will be a leader.' I felt that if I had intelligence and interest, there was nothing I couldn't do. Yale's slogan about graduating 1,000 leaders every year—you could taste that in the air. Now I find competitive situations that I have no idea how to handle."

Most of the graduates have had to take jobs which have nothing to do with their majors and which they find demeaning, if not outright humiliating. Some can find no jobs at all. "In May of my senior year I suddenly realized I not prepared to do anything and nobody at Yale had ever said anything to me about it," another graduate declares. "I was shocked when I got out. I don't regret having gone, but I don't think my education prepared me to be a woman who had to support herself." *

These graduates were not "superwomen"—they were simply very bright girls who had failed to grow up and look around them at the most elementary realities of life. Their families had always provided: why couldn't Yale provide? Why couldn't the college get them an intellectually rewarding job starting at, say, $20,000 a year? *Why isn't somebody taking care of me?*

If these girls had understood—at age eighteen—that *nobody* was going to take care of them any longer, their experience in college would have been vastly different. And they would not have floundered later—wondering why life is so brutal to the young, so unfair to an intellectual, so prejudiced against minorities, so disdainful of a woman's needs. Along with knowledge they would have acquired some common sense, including the insight that college is not in any way a trade school. The intellectual stimulation and cultural enlargement received there may eventually prove valuable even in a material sense, but it is likely to be of little help in getting a job.

* Another graduate felt more grateful to Yale. "My first job was selling 'better blouses' at Saks," she said. "Eighty-five people applied for two positions at the store. The Yale in my résumé got me the job."

We Teach Our Kids That There Is Something Morally Wrong About "Dropping Out" for a While

We are so panicky that, somehow, our children won't end up with a ticket of admission to polite society that all our discussions of college imply a "straight-through" process. But sixteen consecutive years of the same routine is a lot for any human. Yes, the move from home to college is a decided break, but for some kids the change is not enough. They have grown stale with study, and the world of simple, mindless work looks terribly attractive.

As John Adams wrote: "When I was a youth I found myself one day very weary of my studies and asked my father if I might not cease them in favor of other work. He said I might dig a ditch across part of our land which would be useful for drainage. I began with a will, but after two days of this labor under a summer sum I returned to my studies, my mind wondrously clarified as to the difficulty of Latin grammar."

Many high school graduates go on to college because it is the path of least resistance. It requires little effort on their part and it pleases their parents. But education is too precious (and expensive) to waste on the reluctant. If a young adult doesn't really *want* to go to college he should be encouraged to drop out of the educational process until he decides what he does want.

Of course we aren't going to let him stay home and sleep till noon while he thinks about it. Nor will we encourage him to aimlessly wander the planet plumbing the depths of his soul and "trying to get it together." As a young adult he has to support himself. Meditation while performing unskilled labor, as Adams found, does indeed clear the mind as to the alternatives in life. And these days a year of "digging ditches"—even at the minimum wage—can produce money for another assault on formal education or job training, whatever it may turn out to be.

Dropping out in the middle of college may serve an equally

valuable function for our children, and we should let them know early in their teen years that this is an OK way to plan the college pattern. I do mean dropping out to work, of course. Consider these advantages:

❊ A student can test his interest in a career area. One young woman we know says: "It only took me six months as a clerical assistant in a welfare agency to decide that the whole area of social work was not for me. I went back to school and changed my major."

❊ On the other hand, the student may find that he has indeed discovered the field in which he wants to pursue a career. Now he is getting through his "apprenticeship" at a time when it is psychologically easier for him, he is discovering whether postgraduate study will really do him any good, he is gaining work experience which will be useful on his résumé when he goes job hunting, and he is making contacts which will ensure that, when the time comes, he doesn't have to apply "cold" in his chosen field like most of the other graduates. With any luck he may even have a job waiting for him.

❊ To take a break from the educational treadmill and discover the satisfaction of a regular paying job is reason enough, but there may also come a time in a young adult's life when he or she simply has to change environment, for a variety of private reasons. Transfer to another school isn't the only solution; a paying job may be a better place to think out the future.

❊ Last, but hardly least, dropping out to work for a year may be a simple economic *necessity*. Our kids have to be taught from the earliest teen years that they are not underprivileged because we see them as full Adults at Eighteen—and thus the major responsibility for financing their college education lies with them, and not with us.

What? Am I seriously suggesting that my children should pay for their own college education, even if I can afford it? Well, maybe not every penny of it—but certainly they have to assume the basic financial responsibility. There is no doubt in my mind that this arrangement is best for my kids, best for me and my wife, and best for our parent-child relationship. Psychologist Martin Seligman, writing in *Psychology Today*, says:

Many clinicians have reported an increasing pervasiveness of depression among college students. Since this is a generation that has been raised with more reinforcers—more sex, more intellectual stimulation, more buying power, more music, more cars, etc.,—why should they be depressed? Yet the occurrence of reinforcers in our affluent society is so independent of the actions of the children who receive them, the goodies might as well have fallen from the sky.

And perhaps that is our answer. Rewards as well as punishments that come independently of one's own effort can be depressing . . . . To see oneself as an effective human being may require a childhood filled with powerful synchronies between cause and effect, between responding and its consequences . . . . Depression is a belief in one's own helplessness.

When we talk to a child on his thirteenth birthday we have to mean it 100 percent when we tell him the whole adult teaching process is going to end exactly five years from that day. If we don't fully accept this decision ourselves—if we make reservations about cutting all the strings when he's eighteen—then we don't put the necessary emotion and drive into the process, and so the child doesn't really believe it either. He doesn't feel those "powerful synchronies." The whole business becomes a fantasy, a little ritual dance of attitudes and words. We pretend to act tough and our kids learn to maneuver between what we say and what we really mean.

But can't we require them to grow up without cutting them off financially? To put it bluntly, no. Like it or not, money is the ultimate test of reality. How can we regard somebody as independent if we are paying for all his needs? The power of the purse is the power of control. Our Founding Fathers understood that: The executive branch may want to act, but ultimately it must come back to Congress to ask for the money—and modify its conduct until the appropriations committee approves.

No matter how rich and how wise we are, we can't give a lot of money to *anybody* with complete detachment. Even if we declare that the gift is absolute we nevertheless make a silent judgment as to whether the money is being spent wisely. And we find ways, consciously or not, to communicate this judgment to the recipient.

We are so comfortable in our tutorial role as parents that it seems entirely natural and right to influence their actions, in a matter as important as this, especially if we *aren't* rich and we are making the gift at great personal sacrifice. Our judgments, of course, penetrate every aspect of the college student's life. Is he taking the courses that make sense to us? Is he studying hard enough? Is he getting involved with friends in a social atmosphere which might prevent him from studying? Is he drifting into moral attitudes (drugs, sex) which might somehow vitiate the sacrifice we are making? Is he trying hard enough to earn money on his own during vacations? Does he really *need* a car? The list of possible parent-child disagreements is bottomless.

And how does the student react? Often he simply continues the typical teenage passive-aggressive pattern, but with new refinements. Since "getting an education" may not have been truly his idea in the first place (he only agreed to it—an important distinction), and since his parents are still in many ways telling him how to go about it, he finds subconscious means to resist. He takes a "cool" attitude toward teachers who are trying to excite him—the burden of proof that hard study or research is worthwhile lies upon *them*, not him. Often he feels guilty about the sacrifice his parents are making, but then begins to feel angry that he has been made to feel guilty, and the unconscious self-sabotage resumes. Since he also feels frustrated and dependent, he may make a mess of his social and personal relationships. After a time the whole college experience seems negative and meaningless, and he may drop out—creating a family uproar. But more often, college counselors say, kids simply grub on for fear of "letting their parents down." College becomes a prison sentence.

Oh, come now, I'm exaggerating, right? I suppose so, and yet every parent and student will recognize a bit of his own experience here. The parent-child dependent relationship continued through the college years is ambiguous at best and often devastatingly unhappy for both sides. Isn't there a better way? Yes, we seem to have forgotten the old bromide that something free is not highly valued. Or that we take out of an experience only as much as we put into it.

Obviously any student who finances his own college is putting a lot more into the experience and has a completely different attitude toward his studies, his parents, himself, and the world around him.

He may find life harder in the immediate physical sense, but it is infinitely easier in the psychic realm, because the meaning of what he is doing suddenly becomes *clear*. He may make mistakes, but he doesn't feel put down by them, and he learns gladly. He may not work at his full capacity, but he knows why. He has choices to make—choices that are his alone. For the first time in his life he has Power.

We parents have got to get it through our heads that after eighteen years our Power is worn out anyway. We don't have to wait until our kids have graduated from college, married, and moved far away before we can begin to appreciate them as equals. It's a *relief* to give up—perhaps even a joy—and our kids feel it too, and respond to us as never before.

21 ✳

Yes, They Can Do It Themselves

Many parents throw up their hands and say, at today's prices how can my child possibly put himself through college? Even if we wanted him to and he was willing to do it, even if he's bright enough to win scholarships, how could he possibly raise $7,000 a year or $5,000 or whatever it takes these days?

Let's get a clear picture of just how much money is required. The College Entrance Examination Board (the group that administers the SATs) says that for the 1977–78 school year an average student will spend $3,000 on tuition and all living expenses if he goes to a tax-supported college. If he chooses a privately funded school the average cost is $4,900—but this can range up to $7,000 and more for some of the Ivy League colleges and other high-status schools around the country.

Let's hold off considering whether it is *necessary* for your child or mine to go to a $7,000 school during his first four years of college. Let's assume that no matter where he goes we want him to raise $3,000 a year on his own. Can he do it? The answer is yes.

BANK LOANS. 1. Over five million students have taken advantage of the Guaranteed Student Loan Program to borrow directly from a bank *on their own signature*. Most banks will lend at least $1,500 a year, and some will go higher. The federal government, working through a state agency, guarantees repayment of the loan to the bank if the student defaults and it also subsidizes interest, so the total cost is a good deal lower than if the parents had borrowed the money on a straight commercial basis. Repayment begins after the student completes his education and continues for the next ten years.

Should a young person's future be "mortgaged" like this? Good god, our children have a whole life ahead of them; how much "future" do we parents have? To young adults money from a bank is "real" money in a way that parents' funds never are. Bank money has to be paid back, and no student wants to build more debt than he really needs. Nor does he like the idea of cynically planning to declare himself bankrupt to avoid repaying the loan.

Yes, it will be a little hard on him to start payment just as he is beginning his work career; he will have to live fairly lean for a while. But if the payments become too onerous the bank will be sympathetic. No banker wants a default, even if the government will pay, and it is standard practice to stretch out the repayment period as long as a steady effort is being made to retire the debt. What better long-term financial lesson can we give a child than the notion that he has to meet his obligations *before* he improves his standard of living?

A bank loan of $1,500 a year thus provides half of the needed $3,000, but in actual practice it may not be necessary for the student to borrow this much.

2. TEEN SAVINGS. I know a family with six children, all of whom have gone to college and all of whom paid most of their first-year costs from savings accumulated during high school. They worked at after-school, weekend, or vacation jobs because the father told them very early that he could only afford modest assistance for each of them. Were these young people robbed of their carefree youth as a result? No, the kids in this family are a wonder in our town—bright, energetic, and into everything. They got their own jobs, made their own decisions how much to save each year, and still found time to take part in normal teen social activities.

Many parents see the pre-adult years as a kind of Tom

Sawyerish idyll for their children, filled with dreaming, sorting out of feelings, and innocent explorations. Let them alone, we say; they've got the rest of their lives to work. But that isn't how the kids today feel. Teens are *bored* with trying to fill up their time, trying to invent play. They want some significance in their lives and they perceive, dimly, that work is an entry into adult freedom. But, more than anything, some jobs are simply the most *fun* available. It's where the action is. Our Burger King franchise must employ twenty high-school boys and girls, and I never stop in there without marveling how much the kids seem to be enjoying themselves. They aren't fooling around: serving hamburgers and shakes these days is a high-speed production job. These kids are a *team*, they are running the entire operation, and they love it.

In the summer just before his sixteenth birthday Eric got a job at a golf driving range. Some weeks he made as much as $75. He was thrilled at the money, of course, but mainly he was excited because the boss let him drive the giant range tractor which retrieves the balls. My son was still months away from getting his regular driver's license, and I think he would have driven this machine for nothing.

Still, we couldn't believe the money he was coining. Almost unnoticed by us, federal and state hourly minimum wages have been moving up. The legislative intent was to help the poorest of the poor, the blue-collar breadwinner, but the middle-class teenager also benefits. At $2.65 an hour a kid only has to work three nights after school, or one night plus a Saturday or Sunday, to make $25. (Some employers can legally pay teens 85 percent of the minimum wage, but even this adds up.)

Moreover, this income is *tax-free*. The federal exemptions on basic earned income also have jumped sharply. And since we parents don't charge them for board and room the whole $25 may well be discretionary income. They can spend it on any damn-fool thing they want (some *parents* don't have $25 a week in discretionary income). Does a daughter have to blow all her money on cosmetics, records, and clothes fads? Does a son have to fritter his income on pizzas and hopped-up cars? With parental encouragement, they can deposit part of every paycheck into a savings account toward the day they will need it for college.

What is this, you say, the old puritan ethic again? That's right—it's called *thrift*. We underestimate the pride that a teen can feel in saving money for an important purpose, and how responsive adults are when they see this attitude in a young person. One of my business partners could well afford to put her boy through college, but her son chose to work after school and on Saturdays as a supermarket checker—at union wages. He was not a brilliant scholar, but when it came time for the difficult interview with the admissions officer at the only university he wanted to attend, her son had a plan. He emphasized that by his high-school commencement he would have saved enough money to finance his freshman year without help from anyone. I don't have all A's or the top SAT scores, he said, but I know what I want and I'm determined to succeed at it. This wasn't his mother's idea of how to present himself, but it appealed to the interviewer. And, yes, the school did admit him.

If college is supposed to be education for life, the mere effort to get there can make a strong contribution to the educational process. Lisa, too, had picked one of the tough colleges and wasn't sure she had all the credentials necessary—only 20 percent of the applicants were being accepted. We urged her to take extra time and space in her application to permit the Admissions Officer to see her as a person, and not just a statistic. Here is what she wrote about earning money:

Work—and the Capitalistic Society

I have a business of my own, and I do very well at it. I'm an Avon Lady. Why? Baby-sitting and clerking jobs are OK but they don't pay too well on an hourly basis. With Avon I average $4 an hour. I have a very full life with school, music, outside activities and a boy friend, so it is wonderful to have a job in which I control the time and in which my earnings are open-ended. At 17 I'm one of the youngest Avon women in the company.

Avon is not a goof-off job. In order to maintain my 40 percent commission I must average at least $50 per week in sales, or my commission rate drops to 25 percent. I must handle all customer complaints and exchanges, collect my money, and pay my bills. It's hard psychologically—I often have to force myself to go and knock on those doors.

I'm learning a great deal about human nature in the actual selling process, as well as at sales meetings. The world of sales promotion and packaging has its fascinating (and repellent) aspects. It is interesting to observe the mechanisms the company employs to boost sales: "special offers," "unconditional guarantees," and "Avon Fights Inflation" notices. I too am a customer because I must buy all my booklets, samples, and demonstrator items. They employ various devices to improve *my* buying.

Selling does not have the status it once had in America. but I can see there is still a good deal of it (in one form or another) in most kinds of work. I am wiser now for my experience with selling; I am a functioning part of our society—more than most people my age.

Now, those words in themselves don't describe Lisa—this was only one of six parts in which she explained her life and her interests. But they did suggest she was adult enough to see and meet the difficult challenges that higher education presents.

3. LOCAL GRANTS AND SCHOLARSHIPS. At the high school awards assembly in our town (pop. 45,000) nearly $100,000 in grants and scholarships was awarded this year to the graduating class. Some of this money was for special occupational study or was otherwise restricted; some grants, but not all, were limited to students with the greatest need. These scholarships come from a wide miscellany of labor, business, civic, fraternal, and women's groups.

If a teenager knows from a very early age that he's going to need all the help he can get to fund a college education, he may make an effort to discover what the requirements for these awards are. Of course the parents will keep an ear cocked for scholarship opportunities within the community, but the main burden is the student's. At school the obvious starting point is his guidance counselor, but individual teachers and coaches may also know of scholarships available in their field. It's up to the student to persuade one or more school officials to take an interest in him because, for example, he has shown an unusual scientific or mathematical mind, has developed into a demon journalist or creative writer, or has proven to have exceptional talent in art or music. These days there may even be some college athletic scholarships for girls.

To put it bluntly, a kid who has to finance his own college is going to be more involved in the real world at an earlier age, understanding that every action (or lack of action) has a consequence. Outstanding grades, high class rank, and enthusiastic teacher recommendations are not only the key to getting into the college of his choice, they may have considerable impact upon what he does there—and how he pays for it.

4. FINANCIAL HELP FROM THE COLLEGE. Many middle-class parents assume that most available funds are being focused on ghetto youth and other poor with no resources at all. However, a glance through one of the descriptive handbooks on colleges will show that most schools, tax-supported and private alike, offer some kind of help to *between 40 and 50 percent* of their students. A wide variety of assistance is available, ranging from scholarships and outright gifts to loans and student jobs.

This money comes from endowments and/or appropriations by the state legislature, supplemented by federal money available under the National Direct Student Loan Program, administered by the colleges. Most schools don't try to decide themselves just how badly your child may need financial help; they buck the decision to the College Scholarship Service. CSS, a division of the College Entrance Examination Board, bases its decisions on the facts parents swear to in an exhaustive financial report. Since a third to a half of all kids in college end up getting some kind of help through the school, your chances may be better than you think, especially if you have several children in college at once or have had unusual medical expenses in the family or otherwise have had some kind of financial setback.

5. VACATION EARNINGS. CSS assumes that in order to qualify for aid from the college the high school graduate is trying to help himself by working during the summer. A student is expected

to clear $500–600 toward his college costs, which means that a summer job is a necessity, not a way to fill time.

Lisa learned quickly that first summer after high school. Since she was late in getting to Cape Cod, all the good summer jobs had already been filled by college students whose classes had ended weeks earlier. The only work she could find was making beds in a Ramada Inn. Three days later she phoned home that her back was aching so badly that she didn't know if she could stand up straight. She had also acquired an undying respect and sympathy for the working-class women who have few options better than chambermaid.

Two weeks later she had hustled up another job; Lisa was earning $125 a week and more as a waitress in a fine Hungarian restaurant. Although she had never done this kind of work, the family which ran the business liked her well enough to train her and to draw her into the family embrace. Was this a summer of all work and no play? No, during the day she had plenty of time at the beach and soon found a new boy friend. When we went to visit her in mid-August her biggest worry was the bathing-suit consequences of eating all that exquisite homemade strudel.

You probably have your own favorite "summer job" success story. Maybe you heard about the young man who rented equipment from his contractor father and went into business digging excavations for swimming pools; the college girl who convinced a wealthy couple on Long Island that she was a gourmet cook worth $150 a week for the summer; the two boys who went into the house-painting business, lined up their jobs on the spring vacation, and cleared $2,000 apiece for their summer's work; the boy who made over $1,000 shoveling grain on a Great Lakes freighter and found himself in terrific shape for the football squad; the hot-rod tune-up specialist who discovered he was good enough to fill in as a mechanic at a hard-pressed local auto dealer at $8.50 an hour; the two college girls who made peanut fudge and hired a Cub Scout pack to peddle it.

Sure it can be done, even if it simply means helping Uncle

Henry in his floor-waxing business or hiring out as a statistical typist with office temporaries while continuing to live at home. For a bright kid, earning summer money is largely a matter of desire.

6. WORK-STUDY COLLEGES. The psychological and financial advantages of breaking the study grind are so evident that many schools now formally integrate work into the college experience. In the past fifteen years the number of work-study colleges in the United States has expanded from 70 to more than 1,000, and they come in all sizes, systems, and geographical locations.

Northeastern University in Boston, for example, has thirty-four faculty members working full time as placement officers in their fields of specialization. At the moment there are 4,000 full-time students earning good money on the job; they will soon be rotating with 8,000 others currently studying on campus. Generally students work in a field of major interest such as business, engineering, nursing, or teaching, and they take five years to get a degree.

This solves the summer job problem, and it goes a long way toward paying the cost of a college education, as well as finding that first permanent job after graduation.

7. PRIVATE PART-TIME JOBS. An important part of the "financial aid" which any college has to offer is simply a part-time job on campus. This works fine for some kids, helping to cover board and room without too many hours and too much distraction. But others who want better money, more hours, and more satisfying work will look for part-time jobs off campus.

Here too a striking but little-noted economic trend is working in favor of the student putting himself through college. Part-time workers today make up 18 percent of the labor force—a *50 percent* increase in just the last six years. Sears, Roebuck & Co. employs 395,000 people and nearly half now work thirty hours or less a week. Gimbel Brothers in New York has only 40 percent full-time employees, and J. L. Hudson department stores in Detroit 35 percent.

Half of Howard Johnson employees work part time, and 90 percent of McDonald's. Upjohn, the drug company, has 17,000 regular employees and 60,000 part time. Many banks and airlines couldn't get along without part-time clerks. The Travelers Insurance Company in Hartford has 1,400 employees who come in at 6 p.m. for a four-hour mini-shift. Control Data in St. Paul has one plant that hires only part-timers. *Sixteen million Americans today have part-time jobs.*

And it's not all paid at the minimum wage, either. *Forbes* (March, 1977) says the average wage for part-timers is $4.21 an hour, compared to $5.16 for full-timers.

"Kids have to work so much harder in college today than we did," a parent protests. "They really are given tremendously heavy workloads." This may be true in some schools, in some courses, but if so why does a student have to carry a full class schedule? So what if it takes him four and a half or five years to get through college? Are those few extra months going to make a difference?

Some students happily accept the typical adult pattern of work, which means that you find a job you like and you stay with it year around, except for a brief vacation. Laura is a young woman who works five evenings a week as a waitress from 6 to 10 P.M. in a quality restaurant near her college. She carries a reduced course load, but since she continues to work and go to school during the summer she will graduate in the regulation four years. She is doing well in her classes, has an active social life after work and on her days off, gets four weeks' vacation a year, and because the tips are good, has not only put herself through college but by her senior year had saved enough to buy a new car.

No, this pattern may not be attractive to everyone. But it can be done. Laura doesn't have a moment to spare but she feels successful and pleased with her life—more so than most young people her age. Isn't that what it's all about?

8. DROPPING OUT TO WORK. We've already discussed the possibility that there may be times in a student's life when he

knows he simply isn't *functioning* in college. The best therapy could be a spell of simple-minded work. On the other hand, a summer job may open up a fascinating opportunity to gain experience in a career, making it worthwhile from a learning standpoint to stay on for a semester or two. As Mark Twain said, "I never let schooling stand in the way of getting an education."

Bank loans, teen savings, local grants and scholarships, college help, campus jobs, vacation earnings, work-study colleges, private part-time jobs, full-time jobs with a reduced college schedule, dropping out for a time . . . you can surely think of various ways in which students can put themselves through college. Tens of thousands of kids did it in our generation; hundreds of thousands are doing it right now. Why not yours and mine?

22 ✳

Parent Loans: The Last Resort

Of course no parent wants to see his child suffer. Struggle, yes, but not so desperately that he or she loses the larger meaning of the word Education. So, once the principle is established, once a teenager has taken responsibility for his life and his education and resolved the main problems of college financing, a father and mother can afford to relent and help out a little—just as any friend might.

This is especially true for a student who is dead certain he knows what career he wants to pursue. One of the crucial benefits to be gained by self-financing is that it constantly forces a young person to examine what he is doing, and why. But delaying his forward thrust just to make money may be counter-productive if the student already knows what he wants and faces long postgraduate training before he can begin his career, as in medicine and law.

In this case I feel the parents should become the bank of last resort. After the student has obtained all the scholarship help he can, is working as hard as seems reasonable in vacations and otherwise, and has exhausted his borrowing capacity from school and bank, then parents should offer to help, not with a gift but with a formal loan. It should be a legally binding note, typed on an attorney's stationery, bearing interest, and duly witnessed and notarized. To avoid any feeling of manipulation, the funds should be paid out not in a monthly dole but in a lump sum, subject entirely to the student's management. If your son or daughter feels he or she has struggled mightily to make it on his own, you don't want to interfere with that pride.

The repayment provisions in the note can be generous, possibly stipulating that the family loan can wait until the bank debt is satisfied, in the years when the child's income is high and the funds actually might be useful to the parents in their old age. If you have more than one child and hope to maintain your credibility with them, it has to be very clear that the family bank is the court of last resort after all other avenues have been not only explored but well-trod. The other siblings must be reassured that they will not suffer financially if they don't want to become doctors and if they can make it through the four years of their college without tapping the family bank. You can declare that this formal loan will in fact be collected, as far as you are concerned, but in any case will be made part of your will, to be deducted from the borrower's portion of your estate if you should die before the debt is paid.

Does all this seem impossibly hard-nosed and hard-hearted? Make my child sign a legal note before I'll give him money for college? Even Shylock didn't go that far. Am I some kind of monster? No, just a weary parent like you. We have all started out with a hundred grand designs about how things ought to be with our children, but each time the basic principle gets eroded away at the bottom and fuzzed over at the top. Unless we are very clear in our own minds what we want to do, unless we are very *determined* to see it through, unless we believe that it's important for them and not just convenient for us, every project which pushes toward greater maturity and independence falls apart. We are destroyed by sentiment, inertia, fatigue, and refusal to face the consequences of failure.

Here is how I have presented the do-it-yourself college financing program to my children:

"We are not a rich family, but we have enough to live comfortably. We could afford to pay for your college educations, but we aren't going to do it for reasons you understand very well. We have been talking about Adult at Eighteen for a long time, and either we're just kidding or we're for real when we say that we believe in your capacity to grow up and take care of your needs. Most parents and children are frustrated with each other—to say the least. You know quite a few families in which the two generations seem to be at each other's throats. The reason we seem to get along better is that each year it bcomes clearer that you *can* become adult, and you acquire increasing confidence, too. Each year as you become more independent we can take more pleasure and satisfaction in each other.

"Now, your mother and I feel that if we were to put you through college—as most of the parents of other families we know do—we would disrupt the happy process which is developing. You may not entirely agree; you may feel that money has relatively little to do with it. But in any case here's how it is with money in our family:

"Everything that Mom and I have belongs to you, in equal shares. The money that we don't need right now for daily living is what we consider to be a Family Emergency Fund. If anything should ever happen to any of you during your lifetimes, some real trouble physically, mentally, or emotionally, this fund would be available to you, of course, without stint—no matter how old you are. Now, we could dip into this fund to start you off in college, but to tell you the truth we think of college as a part of daily living. We have to pay our mortgage and buy our food at the supermarket, and you as an over-eighteen adult have to buy your food and pay your tuition.

"The most important use of the Emergency Fund will be to take care of us in our old age. Back through history most parents have relied on their children to take care of them when they grew feeble. But we don't intend to do this. Just as we expect you to stand on your own feet at eighteen, we expect to stand on ours for the balance of our lives. Many people we know have to support their parents— just as I had to take care of my mother until she died. Social security is a help, but it isn't enough to live on with any kind of dignity. So it will be a matter of pride with us not to burden you when you have your own families to raise. I think you can see the rough parallel: you have pride now in your independence before your earning power has come to flower, and we'll have pride later when ours has faded.

"Now, since both Mom and I expect to live to be ninety-five, we're going to be budgeting very carefully for these late years. And since it's unlikely that either of us is going to make it, I think you can count on some money being left in our estates for you. So it isn't a question of our being skinflints, of being less generous than other parents, it's merely a question of timing. Our responsibility as parents is to prepare you as best we can for a happy and successful life, and that's what we're trying to do in insisting upon your total independence at age eighteen.

"However, as I said, our surplus funds are to be considered as a Family Emergency Fund. So if one of you runs into a real financial problem he can't handle—for example, if you are embarked on a career which will require years of postgraduate training—then I think you ought to have a right to ask for a loan from the Emergency Fund. But since this money belongs to all of us, the need for the loan ought to be very apparent to all of us, and we ought to call a Family Conference to vote on it."

How do my kids feel about all this? They think it is reasonable and fair. It tells them what they have to do and why, and the money is there if they really need to tap it. They like the idea of pride, too—their pride and ours.

23 ✳

The Real Reason Why
College Is Worth the Effort

If college is no longer absolutely necessary in the economic sense, and if the four years of undergraduate work are of little use as career training, why should our children go to college? Especially if we insist that they make the tremendous effort to pay for it themselves. It seems to me that parents, beginning in the early teen years, have to do a good deal of explaining about the *meaning* of education. This is the position we took in our family:

Education, like virtue, is and always has been its own reward. One of the chief ways in which we differ from animals is our awareness of self, and since each generation can never define itself fully in its own time, we must rely on the accumulated discoveries of man to tell us who we are—and what our future should be. As children we are constantly afraid of a thousand unknowns, and it is only as we grow and educate ourselves that we come to know that these fears are not justified or that most risks are manageable. "Nothing in life is to be feared. It is only to be understood," said Marie Curie. But we have to learn *how* to understand. A poorly educated person constantly feels that life is tossing him about at random—that day after day he is subject to forces which he can never know or control.

Education, however, does not merely bring relief from fear. It

213

is also a positive *joy.* In part this is the thrill of discovery, in part the satisfaction of completion. All our lives we experience tiny pieces of what it is to be a human, and in the early years these are often isolated and baffling occurrences. Suddenly, like the persistent jigsaw-puzzle searcher, we come upon the missing piece which links all the others, enabling us to see the whole picture. This is a crude metaphor, and yet life *is* somewhat of a puzzle; our grandest excitements rise with discovery of the missing pieces.

Again, because man is not a solitary animal, he finds pleasure in education because it leads him to his fellow kind. We choose our lifelong mates and friends not through the casual mutuality of work or play but because of a common identity we discover in our inner lives. In the educational experience we discover a camaraderie of the searchers, and this sets a standard by which we select those we respect and love for the rest of our lives. If the college experience has any validity it shows us how much there is yet to learn and to become, and we can never again be content with those who shut off and mark their lives complete. Education at its best tells us why— and how—to keep on growing.

Of course this message is expressed in small doses in many different ways, and we have to continue to reassure our children after they leave home. When Lisa was a sophomore in college she wrote that many of her friends were dropping out of school and she herself felt discouraged about her courses and her teachers and her ability to cope. What is education all about, anyway? she asked. And does it have to be done in college? Here is part of what I wrote back:

> Education is never completed in college. It is a lifelong process which can only truly begin once you are an adult. Education is not a gift someone else can make to you; it is a gradual accumulation of understandings which everyone has to reach out for and make his own, when and however he can—a very difficult and confusing process. The four years of your undergraduate college may be the only time in your life when anyone

will care enough about you to help you decide what it is you need to learn.

How many different courses does your school offer? I have no idea—it must be hundreds. Think of your undergraduate years as one slow walk down a very long corridor with endless closed doors ranged along each side. Every time you pause to open one door you find a complete world inside, full of light, sound, and movement, and stretching as far as the eye can see. You only have time to venture a few feet into this world as you listen to the resident guide explain what it is that rises before you. Then it's on to the next door and the next little universe. Can you come to *know* these many worlds? Obviously not; the best you can do is to make notes about something you want to pursue in the future.

Nor can you even hope to open more than a fraction of all of the doors on the corridor. When you look at your college catalogue don't you feel frustrated at the many areas of knowledge you will never be able to sample? When you were young you always resisted the totally unknown; the areas of study you liked were the ones you already knew best, and did well in. Young people who haven't grown up continue to walk down the college corridor opening only doors colored pink or green, doors which lead into familiar worlds. But if you accept the idea that the formal educational process is drawing to a close soon, that college could be your last chance for organized guidance, you may be emboldened to open a few strange rainbow-hued doors.

Too many kids walk into a college class and sit down with the same regal air of Louis XV, who said, "Very well, I am here. Astonish me." They expect a professor to put on a show which will engage their attention, if not their enthusiasm, and those professors less skilled in the arts of show business are often written off as dull clods and lousy teachers. Maybe it comes from a lifetime of watching television. (You'd better keep me laughing, friend, or I'll switch channels on you.)

Yes, I will concede that many professors are narrow-gauge

humans, which seems especially sad in an environment totally consecrated to enlargement of the mind and spirit. But that's *their* problem. They have less of an obligation to teach than you have to learn, and this is a critical distinction. It's *your* life you're fiddling around with; if you can't get what you want from them personally, then find other ways to explore for their knowledge.

How much can any one person communicate to another orally, anyway? Do you know that if you read silently the entire script for a half-hour TV newscast you could get through it in less than three minutes? Listening to another person is a waste of time when it comes to absorbing sheer information; you can get it far faster and better organized through a book. Books are written by the best minds—people you will never have personal access to—and every page is well considered and distilled. Our more thoughtful schools are increasingly adopting the European system, which depends less on lectures than on organized individual reading under the guidance of a tutor.

What purpose does a teacher serve, then? First of all, he makes a gift of his *passion*. Every college student is so inundated with areas of knowledge to be explored that he or she has trouble setting priorities of time and effort. Of course we seek an emotional as well as cerebral payoff in our learning, and a live professor gives us some clue as to what we can hope for. (If *he's* so excited, maybe this course is worth an extra effort on my part.)

Secondly, he can offer playback. The author of a book can only try to anticipate questions in a general way; he can't satisfy your specific curiosity. Nor can he require you to summarize your reading—prove that you truly understand it—by writing it down on a piece of paper. Yes, final exams are often poorly conceived by the professor and offer little real opportunity to demonstrate mastery of the material covered. But again, this is *his* problem—if you read the book, did the work, then you got the benefit.

All too soon you are out of college, and nobody is requiring you to study anything but your job. This is a great relief at first, but the scope of first (or even second) jobs is often shockingly limited. Quite often you will have your evenings and your weekends totally free. Right now that sounds like heaven, but surprisingly soon you find a vague hunger rising. The work demands too little of you, and the pleasures of your free time finally become repetitive and cloying. You begin to sense that you have settled into the final pattern of adult life, and it's not as liberated and exciting as you thought it would be. It is, above all, lacking in the constant mental challenge and stimulation you are so used to. Out of sheer boredom you begin to read, and perhaps you sign up for an "adult education" course here and there.

An educated person is defined by the range and depth of his curiosity. The more we learn of the world, the less satisfied we become with what we already know. The pursuit of understanding, I am happy to tell you, becomes easier and more pleasurable as you go along, because each year you have more to bring to the quest. You not only have a greater accumulation of reading and study but also increased *experience* to help put it all into proportion. Perhaps most important of all, we bring a new and stronger *attitude* toward the educational process.

Despite my insistence that you are an adult at age eighteen, this of course is impossible. Full adulthood is composed of a hundred thousand masteries, and none of them are achieved at any particular date. Each human grows in a bizarrely individual way, and there are certain qualities and strains within us which are locked away at some primitive, childlike level. In the late teens and early twenties of the college years most people are still very unevenly developed; the simple process of living life a few more years tends to round us out. If you have ever met someone who has gone back to college in his forties or fifties you will know what I mean; the physical labor of cogitation may be greater, but these people have so much more to bring to each area of study that their pleasure is apparent. They almost always get good grades as a matter of course.

My point is that you *will* want to continue your self-education, and the effort doesn't get harder. If there is some area which you find especially difficult right now, don't worry about it. For example, although I never took a course in Russian novelists, I twice tried to read *War and Peace* while I was in college. Several years after I graduated I remember trying again; once more I bogged down in too many characters, too many canvases, too many Russian patronymics. Suddenly when I was thirty I picked up the book again during my vacation and swept through it with absolute ease and delight in two days. I was astounded; how could I have had such a hard time earlier?

The world of the mind is strange and constantly fulfilling in new ways, dear daughter. I greatly hope you can see college not as some dreadful purgatory to be shuffled through before you can start your life, but as itself the beginning of the best that is to come.

24 ❊

Adult at Eighteen:
What's in It for <u>Us</u>?

Seneca said, "No man counts himself great if his children have failed."

When he is young, a man wants the whole world, and everything in it. Together with his wife, he constructs a dream and works hard to make it real; quite often he is successful. But somewhere in his late thirties or early forties he pauses to take stock. He can begin to see the final shape of his career and he asks himself how much more of the world's powers and pleasures he really needs. Especially if they require him to give second priority to the human element in his life, which provides the most lasting satisfaction.

Quite likely he has left the major burden of raising the children to his wife. But now, with his life half gone, he suddenly sees and feels them not only as his claim to immortality but also, whether he likes it or not, as a certain measure of who and what he is. He begins to sense that even if his career successes have not totally matched his dreams, he will feel reasonably good about his life if his children turn out to be happy and productive humans. And conversely, as the old Roman said, if his children don't fulfill themselves, his life will take on a bitter aftertaste, no matter how splendid his own achievements.

219

Whether or not she also has been involved in a career, his wife will certainly share these sentiments now. Unfortunately, the teen years are likely to be the most difficult period in their children's lives. Often every aspect of the parent-child relationship appears to be going wrong, just at a time when the parents most want things to go right.

In these teen troubles we don't seem to find a lot of outside help; even kindly Dr. Spock can't assure us that the Terrible Thirteens will automatically turn into the Faintly Charming Fourteens. "Adult at Eighteen" is not a formula, either. But it's a *starting point* at which parents can organize their thinking. If we work back from a child's eighteenth birthday we can begin to see where we are and can create some kind of framework to guide future action. Every family is so different, of course, that I couldn't be more specific in these pages. But think back to the basic ideas expressed in our family experience:

✧   Reduce the level of conflict by giving up trying to control areas which are not important to the emotional life of the family.

✧   Express love to each child every day—by words, deeds, and physical contact.

✧   Make it clear to each child that you really mean it when you say you have a five-year plan to transfer all power—and show the child where he or she stands at each stage of the plan.

✧   Hold regular family conferences to reopen silted channels of communication, to permit the teen to air grievances, and to give you better information as to whether the plan is working.

✧   Make a commitment to change, to practice what you preach, and to allow the children to show you where you are wrong.

What does Adult at Eighteen do for us as parents? It relieves the terrible frustration of standing by watching things go sour. We all have more wisdom than we realize in handling our children if we can envision, in slightly more concrete terms, where we are trying to take them.

As indicated earlier, the Adult at Eighteen concept may also help us to restructure our middle years in ways which are more satisfying and beneficial. For example, if a father did not see the need to accumulate an enormous store of after-tax dollars to pay for his children's long years in college, he might well follow a different career path. He might move into a job he liked better—certainly he wouldn't have to push so hard for advancement. Yes, some men would do it anyway, just because it was possible; but some *wouldn't.* Some men would feel freer to refuse a transfer or promotion or a job that required constant travel, if this diminished them as a human being and as the father of a family.

If they could see an absolute end to their financial commitment, some men would not only "ease up" but actually retire earlier, because the money they had accumulated could be used as a cushion for old age. (I know a man sixty-four years old who says he has put five kids through college and is only now starting to lay something by for his old age. He has a good tennis game and I'd like to play with him oftener—but he can't spare the time.)

Many men make a mistake in their choice of careers, but at the age of forty they feel it's too late for a change. How can they possibly start over in a job or a business that pays *less* money—in the face of all that college tuition? In their drive to the top many men also develop an enormous set of false values—they feel they should acquire expensive possessions, for one thing. This is rationalized on the basis that they are providing well for their families. But when there suddenly *isn't* any family any more, in the financial sense anyway, when a man and his wife are alone with their luxury and status, they often look at each other and ask: What do we need all this for? At this point, Life should, and can indeed, begin again.

Everybody in this country is getting liberated except father, especially the middle-class father. He's got to give himself permission to stop pushing so hard for so long. To pull back his financial deadlines by four years may be important in saving him from a heart attack or some other physical breakdown, but at the very least this is going to improve the quality of his life. A man less harassed has time and psychic energy to inject himself into the real life of the family. He's *there* in the critical years when his teenagers are making go or no-go decisions. A man who likes himself better likes his wife better, and his children. The wife thus functions at a higher level as a mother, because she doesn't feel so abandoned in her job of raising the kids. She has more courage to stand up to the tough decisions which a teen forces on the family if she knows her husband truly stands beside her.

Few men have a plan for the middle years of their life. Everything revolves around the job, but who can forecast the progress of a career with any precision? If, however, a man starts from the premise that he's got to be very involved on the home front during the years when his children are thirteen to eighteen, these are exact dates. And if he makes up his mind that he has only minor financial obligations to his children once they reach eighteen, he can also see fairly clearly what his money needs are going to be in the coming years. The driving imperatives of his work thus begin to take shape.

As a skilled manager he ought also, with a great deal of love, to help his wife in her struggle to reassert her identity as an adult, independent of the mothering role. Some women can go back to work while their children are still home and others quickly move outside the home in other ways; but not every woman can lead two lives to her satisfaction. If a husband plans to go on living with this woman, he has to help her start thinking what she is going to do and *be* for the rest of her days after the kids are gone.

Many a mother has a psychological stake in not seeing her children grow up too soon. If she has been focusing most of her intelligence and emotions on the kids, if fulfilling their needs is her major source of self-respect, she obviously senses a great crisis time ahead. For some women the peak years are those when they are the most needed, when the children are small and demanding. Every teen birthday reminds them that a mother's function is less vital. By the time the last child reaches eighteen, these women may still be in their early forties, with nearly *forty years* yet to live. Every woman knows she's got to make some major changes in her life then, perhaps resuming a career or "getting involved" in other work. At the very least, she has to restructure and perhaps rebuild her relationship with her husband. For some women the physical symptoms of menopause are minor compared to this trauma, and it's understandable that they unconsciously postpone the pain as long as possible.

But our teenagers have a keen eye for role models. Why should they not reject us if father seems to be an absentee human, eternally money-grubbing at a job he doesn't particularly like, and mother has become an intellectual dingbat who can be manipulated and ignored, who doesn't appear to have any identity or drives of her own, and increasingly fears she can't cope with the world outside her home? Why should they want to be like us? Why should they consider our values?

The most immediate benefit of Adult at Eighteen is that it forces us to develop a plan during our children's chaotic teen years, so that we can channel some of our parental fears into concrete action. But beyond this it requires parents to start thinking once more about who *we* are and where we're going. Life may not begin again at forty, but it certainly renews itself when we stop seeing ourselves primarily as Mom and Dad. If we can "let go" with reasonable confidence, a child's eighteenth birthday becomes the first day in the rest of our lives, too.